TEACHING ART TO YOUNG CHILDREN 4-9

TEACHING ART TO YOUNG CHILDREN 4-9

Rob Barnes

School of Education, University of East Anglia

London
UNWIN HYMAN
Boston   Sydney   Wellington

Unwin Hyman,
15–17 Broadwick Street,
London W1V 1FP, UK

Unwin Hyman, Inc.
8 Winchester Place, Winchester, Mass. 01890, USA

Allen & Unwin (Australia) Ltd,
8 Napier Street, North Sydney, NSW 2060, Australia

Allen & Unwin (New Zealand) Ltd in association with the
Port Nicholson Press Ltd,
60 Cambridge Terrace, Wellington, New Zealand

First published in 1987
Second impression 1988

British Library Cataloguing in Publication Data

Barnes, Rob
    Teaching art to young children 4−9.
1. Art—Study and teaching (Elementary)
I. Title
372.5′044   N350
ISBN 0−04−371096−4
ISBN 0−04−371097−2 Pbk

Library of Congress Cataloging in Publication Data

Barnes, Rob, 1944−
    Teaching art to young children, 4−9.
Bibliography: P.
Includes index
1. Art—Study and teaching (Primary)—England
I. Title
N365.G7B35   1986   372.5′044   86−8032
ISBN 0−04−371096−4 (Alk. paper)
ISBN 0−04−371097−2 (Pbk.: Alk. paper)

Set in 10 on 12 point Century Old Style
and printed in Great Britain by
Biddles, Guildford

To C.

Contents

―――――― 1 ――――――

Making Links

1

―――――― 2 ――――――

The Value of Art

8

Learning to See, Art and the Individual,
Art as an Expression of Feeling, Deciding on What to Value

List of Illustrations

Colour Plates

Monochrome Illustrations

Charts

Acknowledgements

Particular thanks are expressed to all those teachers and students who over the years have helped form the ideas contained in this book. It is not possible to mention them all by name but special thanks must be extended to Dinah Birnie, Mavis Eccles, Sheila Gillies, Claire Goodman, Norman Manners, Ann Meades, Liz Molander, Mary Mundey, Amanda Parker, Jill Shea, Molly Turner, Sylvia Turner and Julie Whyte. Grateful thanks are also due to the staff and children of Catton Grove First School, Clover Hill First School, Heartsease First School, Ipsley First School, Knowland Grove First School, Lakenham First School, Lyng C.P. School, Northfields First School and West Earlham First School.

Six children, whose work has been collected over a period of time, deserve special mention. They are Adam Ballard, Richard and Peter Barnes, Rebecca Bryant, Toby Whalen and Mary Wright.

For her tireless constructive help and support during the writing of this book, special thanks are due to Cathy Whalen.

Foreword

All aspects of education should be questioned for their relevance in the curriculum. Long-established activities can become a tradition or habit but not necessarily fulfil the needs of children and the community. In writing this book Rob Barnes explains and justifies the wide range of concerns which are at the heart of education, with clarity and depth. Many aspects of the subject are covered theoretically and with sound practical ideas and advice.

Art provides us with a prime means of learning, understanding and communicating. In this way it is significant across the curriculum. Without the skills involved, our children can be denied access to extensive areas of knowledge and the opportunity for individual responses.

Teaching is a creative process and in art and design activities the approach of the teacher is critical. We can teach by supplying set pieces for our pupils to imitate or we can create situations in which pupils develop self-confidence, working on the basis of their own experience, extending their understanding, discovering, satisfying their curiosity and gaining pleasure. The good teacher will accept children, whatever their ability, and will harness and enhance their imaginative and natural talents.

Rob Barnes's understanding of the needs of children and his sensitivity to their individuality enable him to suggest an extensive range of approaches to the teaching situation. These provide a rich source of guidance and stimulation for anyone involved with children. For the thoughtful reader this book can be the source of reassurance and satisfaction as a teacher and ensure relevance and pleasure for the pupils.

Norman Manners

Norman Manners
Chairman, Association of Advisers in Art and Design
Senior Adviser (Art and Design)
Norfolk Education Authority

1

Making Links

TO BE involved in creative activity is to confront how we feel about things. Expressing a mood, emotion, or temperament through art becomes as valid as responding to another person, a moving sight, or a meaningful experience. Both responding and expressing through art puts us in touch with qualities which are part of what makes us human. As such they give special significance and meaning to what we see with our eyes and the inner eye of the mind. They touch on part of us that nothing else can.

For children, art can be a means whereby they reconstruct and assimilate the experiences they have had. What might have been an incomplete inner vision can become clear enough for them to give meaning to what they encounter and can help to build up concepts of themselves in relation to the world. Nowhere is this more obvious than when young children cannot read or write. Their early art provides them with a personal language which describes the world they live in through the shapes and symbols they make when they draw. By adult standards those symbols are often poorly executed, even inadequate, but they are unique to the child who did them and crucial to his development. Clumsy and primitive the drawings may be, but they record an experience of perception and a stage reached in a child's personal growth and awareness.

Most of us who are teaching would want to help this process and try to find ways of developing children's artistic learning. By intuition we might find our way. More likely we would briefly rub shoulders with theories of art education and develop our own teaching partly through our own practice, partly through contact with other teachers and the work they do. Some of the theory could be hard going and some of the practice meaningless to us, especially if we were only presented with finished pieces of children's work to puzzle over. Making links between principles and practice has traditionally proved difficult. In art teaching, an ethos of apparently vague and random objectives characterizes many classrooms. It could be argued that the teachers should make these links for themselves but that would be to ignore the problems most of us have in putting theory into practice. An understanding of principles, the essential part of any theory, does not automatically lead to good practice. Nor does good practice mean that principles of art teaching are understood.

It is not difficult to find children enjoying their artwork, coping with what we asked them to do and controlling materials. But how do we know if they are really learning anything? Are they engaged in anything worthwhile? Painting a cardboard box bright red all over may be enjoyable. It may be interesting, but has it any educational value to the child so industriously occupied in doing it?

The themes in this book are intended to bring together principles and practice so that effective art teaching can evolve. Practical examples are set against principles encountered in issues such as how children draw, problem solving, producing original artwork, and what value art offers. Like most views on art and design, the arguments and suggestions set down here can undoubtedly be challenged. Art thrives on its multiplicity of viewpoints and its unwillingness to be governed by any hard and fast rules. For that reason, conceptual models have been avoided in favour of arguments which try to touch more on the experience of teaching art than on its various theories. The intention is to examine principles and practice together rather than try to separate them entirely. A frequently made assumption is that the two can successfully be divided and analysed. Yet though one may be associated with thinking, the other with doing, they are not necessarily separable nor do they always prove to be helpful by being treated in this way.

Another, and perhaps less obvious, aim is to discuss art teaching in a context of 'creative teaching'. Teachers are far more creative in their thinking than they often suspect, and art can be a way of using this creativity across the whole curriculum. To that end, many ideas in this book will be found to cover a far wider range of curricular interests than art alone.

Not many decades ago we would have believed that art was for a few gifted children. Nowadays, the majority of children are regarded as being creative and their artwork is readily cited as evidence of their creativity. The shift in viewpoint has partly resulted from the influence of a variety of educationists as well as changes in the way we see our roles as parent and teacher. In Victorian times, children were viewed as imperfect adults, now they have qualities which we recognize make them perfectly childlike and capable of producing imaginative 'Child Art'. They are no longer seen as inadequate small adults but as being able to produce artwork with special qualities which no adult could hope to emulate. We expect children to be taught as individuals as well as being part of a

Figure 1   A Thinking Face. Age 6. 370 x 500 mm

group, and we have organized our education system so that individual learning is valued.

We also expect that children will do more in their artwork than just copy. Deliberately to teach children to copy would not fit any principle of individual learning or creativity and we would rightly think a narrow way of working had been prescribed. Some principles are already formed in our minds and affect how we approach teaching art. Others need to be understood so that we can set activities in an appropriate educational context. From sound principles we can then plan children's work more purposefully so that it promotes their learning, besides just being enjoyable.

To impose one view of art teaching would be a fruitless exercise. We still have every right as teachers to choose where we stand. Children learn successfully despite experiencing different methods of art teaching. The very differences we see in good practice only reflect the variety of excellence which is possible. For that reason the examples which appear in this book should be treated with some caution and carefully considered rather than blindly accepted as good or bad. A lot depends on the perceptions we bring with us and these inevitably influence our preference for working one way rather than another.

What works for one teacher may not work for us. But examples, such as the one which follows, have a knack of illuminating our own views by their realistic and concrete nature, even if they do not coincide with our own preferences. A slight shift of principle or practice often arises when one particular way of working has been found wanting. And in this example, the effect on children's work was considerable, the change of tack a result of personal choice.

> I used to think of providing different things for children to do each day. Then I discovered you really have to listen to them talking about their experiences so you can get them to record and extend their thinking. They must use ideas from things they themselves experience at first hand. They need to handle things because at this age, tactile experience is very important. If they can feel and experience for themselves they produce work of far greater vitality than if I'd planned what they should do and forced it on them.
>
> (First school headteacher)

In choosing to work from one principle rather than another we are bound to be guided by what succeeds. But how are we to know what good practice is? We could be told that this or that piece of work demonstrated good practice and try to emulate the examples. But we would be no better than the pupils we criticize for copying. The successful art teachers are often those who have discovered ways of developing their own ideas without resorting to copying those of the teachers they see around them. Ideally, each of us should gain enough understanding about art teaching to know what we are looking at and assess if anything is being learned by the child who painted his bright red box.

Even the intuitively good teacher will talk about artwork in a way which eventually reveals she is working from firmly held principles. She may be unable to analyse her own teaching, yet determined to produce original work, or to give guidance without being over-directive. Or she may want her pupils to be problem-solvers in their artwork.

> We were discussing mazes and this led on to a lot of work in drama ... we acted out what it was like to go through a maze ... what you might meet along the way. Then the children went on to draw their own mazes. They could choose from a variety of drawing materials and I told them the mazes had to function ... they could choose whether or not to draw them out in rough first. We discussed hedges and whether they might meet good or bad things in their maze. One boy drew his mum as a good thing to meet ... there were a lot of pots of gold and some children saw mazes as patterns to be embellished. They're used to decorating things because I teach a great deal through pattern, so it's not very surprising that they bring it into their mazes.
>
> (Teacher of 6-year-olds)

From what is said, and from the illustrations (Figure 2, Plate 2), we know that a principle operating is that children are expected to come up with their own solutions. There is some link with previous experience of patternwork and we know the topic of mazes crosses subject barriers. The teacher is also concerned that the children choose from a wide variety of drawing materials. We also sense that the work in progress is inventive and contains a design problem, one which makes children think artistically when they embellish it with pattern.

What we do not know is how the maze project came to be planned and developed. Even if she appeared to work spontaneously, the teacher's frame of reference and understanding of art teaching was clearly crucial. In the example she began by involving her children in drama, then art. She linked the two and indicated a principle of her own art teaching by allowing children to choose materials. But we are given only a glimpse of her teaching process, rather as if we have been invited too late into the classroom. We may be intrigued or even impressed by the end-products we see, but are left ignorant of most of the attitudes which permeate her work.

Figure 2   Maze Picture. Age 6. 300 x 210 mm

End-products do not readily reveal principles in the same clear way that a financial statement produces a balance of figures. We could analyse some forms of artwork to our heart's content without discovering anything more momentous than the fact that paint was mixed thickly or thinly. Understanding principles and how they link with practice is a task associated more closely with processes than with puzzling over finished artwork as if it held the ultimate key.

Fortunately we are not wandering through a maze trying to find pots of gold along the route. We already bring to art teaching our own experience and perception. There must be very few teachers who do not regularly see children occupied in drawing or painting, or who have never tried it out for themselves. Even if the experience was limited, art teaching need not remain the province of a specialist or artistically gifted teacher. There is plenty of good art teaching being done by teachers whose own artistic abilities are slight. Many of them give their children confidence through joining them in learning what art is all about rather than setting themselves apart as experts. Their understanding grows as they develop expertise from uncertain but potentially promising beginnings.

To be uncertain is a feature of much creative thinking. How else would we break new ground or have a single original thought? Yet from uncertainty can grow a genuine confidence in working creatively with children and a surprising discovery of their ability to amaze us with their innocent originality. They will inevitably teach us a great deal about art through what they produce. But we are also in a position to create the best possible climate for their creative work to evolve. Almost all we need as a starting point is a mind open to the persuasion that art has value. From there we can encourage, motivate and guide children in what for many of them will be a lasting and influential early experience of art.

Figure 3

2

The Value of Art

If the teacher does not concern herself with helping children learn what is important in the arts, there is little reason for children to believe that the arts have something worth learning.

(Eisner, 1972)

ANY VALUE that art might have in the eyes of our culture is something that has to be the concern of schools, as well as the rest of society. Otherwise we ignore what makes us human. Art is part of the human condition and contrasts sharply with our more specific needs to invent things and make discoveries through technology. Art does not function in the same sense that technology has produced for us the micro chip computer. Artistic values are less concerned with function and more associated with what they do for us in a learning, civilizing and enriching capacity. As such they are easily called into dispute, largely because they deal with immeasurable qualities, often because they defy conclusive proof. If we are to be convinced by arguments for the value of art then our yardstick is more one of human experience than scientific testing.

From the beginning of our existence we have needed to make forms which express the values which make us human beings whose imaginative gifts distinguish us from other animals. The silicon chip is no substitute for our imagination and senses, and throughout the centuries art has been practised to articulate, refine and give expression to our visual sense.

The evidence of art in galleries and buildings across the world points to a fundamental need in us to make visual expression of who and what we are. In more recent times our education has been as much to do with the way we live, our relationships and judgements, as it has with our intellectual understanding. The notion of an educated person rests not solely with scientific and intellectual achievement. In the final analysis we might hold our wisdom and ability to make good judgements more valuable as assets in a civilized society. At the end of the fifteenth century we could hardly have claimed that Leonardo da Vinci's scientific achievements were the sum total of his fame or education. He expressed his worth through art as well as science in that rare combination which makes for genius (Perry, 1973).

How would he have fared in today's English primary school with its tradition of the three Rs? For one thing, it is unfortunate that he would find in so many schools that art is a low-status subject which is often done to keep children busy, or bring about a mildly therapeutic effect. For another, he would discover that where teachers really believe in the value of art they often have to fight hard to justify its importance for children's learning. There are many teachers who are ready to champion a one-sided set of intellectual values and see art as providing for the emotions and nothing more. If they think that schools are entirely for developing the intellect, then it doubtless becomes very hard to make a good case for art's inclusion as a subject in the curriculum. Fortunately the fight for its inclusion as a subject in our schools was won long ago. But if its place alongside basic subjects is to be fully realized we must look carefully at what value it has.

Learning to See

Children may be literate in the usual sense of the term, but development of visually sensitive or visually literate children is a fundamental reason for doing art. If we understand that literacy means we can read and write, it can also be applied in art to looking and drawing. Of course artists do far more than look and draw. To develop an awareness of and receptivity to visual things includes all the things we associate with artistic pursuits. Artists, for example, invent, imagine and analyse, as well as apply colour, sculpt and assemble things. But all these activities contribute to what educates children artistically by making them literate in a particularly visual way.

Through a sharpened visual sense they learn to see much more and to see with greater insight than they otherwise would. For them, trees which were rather generalized perceptions become objects of close observation and significance. They become personal and special to the child as viewer of them. The flight of a bird, the form of a sea shell, or the twisted roots of a tree, all have aesthetic qualities which visual literacy makes it possible to experience. And part of becoming visually aware is for children to discover the enjoyment of being able to see with the eye of the artist who is awake to the appearance of the surrounding world. By developing the ability to see in far more specific ways, children can begin to disregard what is merely superficial and allow themselves to become attentive to the more subtle qualities and changes of form which are present in everything their eyes and minds rest on.

The close attention that children can bring to looking allows them to concentrate on much more than each form in isolation. When their visual sensitivity is undeveloped they tend to focus on one thing at a time and draw quite separate objects surrounded by space. Art can help them to perceive the world in a greatly extended way so that they then begin to assimilate a variety of perceptions in relation one to another. What was previously placed as an object in a drawing on its own can gradually become part of a complete network of related shapes. With a heightened perception, usually when children are older, the paper is often treated more as a whole and the content is organized to include combinations of objects together.

At the heart of perception, according to what Arnheim (1966) believes, is expression. What he says is that before we perceive in an analytical way, we perceive the expressive or feeling-character of things. He describes this as a skill necessary for survival when we respond to facial expression to determine how friendly or hostile other people are. We can imagine instances when children are more aware of the expressive character which objects display than of what they actually are. Some objects become frightening and others lovable through children's perception of them. And in this, the expressive characteristics of what they experience play an undeniable role in their relationship to them, and in the way they incorporate them into their artwork.

Without our developing visual literacy the rather commonplace remains so. Most people at some time or another have picked up stones from a beach and flung them into the sea for the pleasure of doing something quite useless. Sooner or later they will pick up a stone and examine it for its rounded form or its qualities of colour or decoration.

Such awareness develops when we have the time to stop and look at things for ourselves. But in the classroom we have the chance to develop this perception much further by deliberately making time for looking at things through the process of art.

The qualities that an object like a beach pebble can convey are an important part of its whole character. Though children will examine their world in a variety of other ways, such as by measuring and describing in words, their visual discrimination of things is vital to their ultimate understanding of them. No amount of words can really describe an irregular shape quite so accurately as a drawing does. And the way children interpret everyday objects through drawing is often far superior to their looking at photographs. Even if we discount for the moment any expressive, artistic qualities drawings have, as a way of making children look closely they are unique. Biologists will quickly point out that photographs do not very adequately convey the structure of things but drawings can provide an interpretation which is scientifically sound as well as instructive.

It is true that before the age of 6 years, children tend to draw what they know rather than what they see. But in a class of 6 year-olds there can regularly be a great deal of searching drawing going on, which is as much hard work as anything else they do. Learning to see is rarely something children find easy, and as one teacher says,

> This idea that art isn't hard work is a fallacy. When they're really working hard at drawing, some of them find it very difficult just as they find language and number difficult. I've made them look long and hard many times at the shape of things around them and now none of them say 'I can't draw', any more than they say 'I can't read or write' ... They were drawing these sticky buds and it was fascinating to listen to them talking to each other about their drawings and saying things like 'Look, it's got a horse-shoe shape on it. Is that why it's called a Horse Chestnut?' ... all this talking ... a lot of language work comes out of it ... someone describes the outside of the buds as being like toffee ... they're engrossed in looking and analysing what they see.

The same teacher spoke about the frustration some of her children experience when they draw.

> I have one little boy who's very good at drawing but some days he will get so frustrated that he leaves his drawing unfinished. He doesn't want to see it again. Other days he is so carried away with what he is doing his face is a picture of joy. Some days it goes well, some days it doesn't.

In that sense, art is no different from the rest of the curriculum. Yet it presents children with the task of dealing with special visual qualities that no other subject offers. The ability to perceive those qualities is bound to emerge over a long period of time and is a result of a necessary repeated involvement in art. As we grow up we learn to discriminate between more complex qualities than ever a child can, and may even become like a connoisseur or specialist in certain specific judgements. The wine connoisseur, for instance, is a good example of the development of a sharpened sense of taste for wine. He spends the time needed to refine his experience of tasting wines and bases his judgement partly on previous known good wines he has sampled. Through art, we begin to see qualities which have visual subtlety, such as the many shades of colour to be found in a field of grass, patterns made by clouds in the sky, the different colours to be found in brickwork, or the variety of shapes in fallen leaves. Dewey (1934) in *Art as Experience* said,

> To think effectively in terms of relations of qualities is as severe a demand on thought as to think in terms of symbols, verbal and mathematical. Indeed since words are easily manipulated in mechanical ways, the production of a work of genuine art probably demands more intelligence than does the so-called thinking that goes on among those who pride themselves on being 'intellectuals'.

Attending to special qualities which things have includes not only what children take in with their eyes but what they eventually give out in their art. Through using art materials children learn to deal with colour, shape, line, texture and tone (by which is meant the lightness and darkness of things). These formal elements of art are a constant source of wonder to children who are motivated to explore art media to see what they are like. Even though they must look first in order to create anything, it naturally is not long before the artwork itself demands their close attention, just as their surroundings have done. In turn, attention to the subject matter or content of artwork, the lines, the colours and the shapes, is helped and hindered by the materials which are used. The resulting work is a compromise between what the artist wants to do and what the medium will actually allow. Those qualities which Dewey speaks of constantly present themselves as the children try to interpret the world through their artistic thinking and the media they use.

There is value just in being confronted by new and different materials. Left to their own devices, children might by chance use a variety of media, but the sensitive art teacher can ensure that they find out about, and make comparisons between, the nature of different materials. This can be approached through problem-solving (see Chapter 12) and, for young children, by means of structured play. Practice in handling various materials is part of any young child's education. Observing the world is not enough. Handling materials and finding out what they do demands a different kind of thinking and the development of a variety of physical skills.

This is very apparent when children use clay or Plasticine. Three-dimensional materials pose a different set of problems to solve from the two-dimensional ones of flat paper and drawing. A child working on paper organizes the world into two-dimensional symbols. But using clay gives children the opportunity to mould and express a three-dimensional world in a three-dimensional way.

Children become more fluent in their creative ideas the more often they tackle creative projects. Like success breeding success, fluency can be a feature of continual involvement in creative thought. Children can learn to rely on quite illogical thought processes to arrive at new solutions. Trusting in what may amount to intuition or good guesses can be bad practice in an intellectual process of thought. But in the arts it is more or less a way of life, and for children, a valuable way of coping with the qualities of life which refuse to submit to rational or intellectual thought.

A long-term aim of developing visual literacy is to make children so aware of their surroundings that they go on looking when they grow up. The richness of nature, for instance, can be experienced through art precisely because of art's appropriateness as a way of knowing the world. Developing visual sensitivity, we can argue, is important for producing artistically educated and aware adults who actually care what the things around them look like. There is of course nothing wrong with being trained to earn a living but this is hardly the same as being educated. Without art being taught in schools, we can imagine children being less open to artistic enrichment in later life than they are now. Or if they were open to appreciating art, the judgements they might make would be founded more on ignorance than on knowledge and awareness.

To talk about art as a way of knowing suggests that what we are dealing with is a form of intelligence. The idea is not new (see Witkin, 1974; Ross, 1983). Or if not intelligence itself, then it is a code we have developed so that we can understand reality as it exists for us. We see things not as they are, but as we are. The private code of artistic sensitivity becomes our window for viewing reality and for each one of us

A creature with forty-nine heads.

Figure 4   Creature from *James and the Giant Peach*. Age 6. 750 x 480 mm

it can be as different as Chinese and English are as languages. In Chinese some words do duty both for nouns and verbs so that objects are also events that are happening (Watts, 1957). This is confusing to Western minds but what is apparent is that the perception of reality differs for all of us according to the particular way of knowing we develop. For children, art is not meant merely to be an alternative way of knowing, but is part of the way they learn to trust what their senses tell them.

Where subject areas in schools are blurred, as they often are for young children, to treat art as a separate and unconnected way of knowing is to deny its effect on other forms of learning. Children need to be involved in art to complete their understanding of what they see and to educate the visual sense, not only for producing art, but for learning in a rounded and meaningful way. Support for this view comes from the 1978 HMI Primary Survey. This said that the general progress of children and their competence in basic skills appeared to benefit where they were involved in a programme of learning which included art in its list of activities.

Quite simply, the development of a visual sense seems to make children more alive and identified with the world. Whenever we learn something new our way of knowing the environment is transformed. We have gained awareness we previously did not have. Children who are alive to their world often display a curious exploratory and adventuresome spirit. They are 'participators' in life whose knowledge, gained through a variety of subjects, spurs them on to know more. They may not grow up to be creators of art later in life, but if they cannot become artists, they can at least learn to appreciate the art that other adults do.

It might be said that wisdom is acquired rather than received. Each of us has to construct our own fundamental concept of what it means to learn to see. Immersed in the making of images and objects, it is easy to lose sight of what art offers as a way of comprehending the world. Art encourages us to understand and give meaning to what we see. Perhaps as old men and women we will remember only what had meaning for us, what we learned about life and what deeply affected us. We will certainly include what we saw and if we are lucky may even be aware that changes took place in our visual perception of things. The trees we drew, the plants, the houses, the people, all affected our perceptions of them.

If children look carefully enough, the object they draw can change their private ignorance of its appearance. Pablo Picasso once said, 'I do not seek, I find.' This describes learning to see very well. Through a heightened perception, a well-developed habit of seeing, children can move from 'looking' to 'finding' without always needing to be directed to do so. The fact that they have developed the habit of seeing has wider implications and may well influence the whole of the rest of their curriculum. We do not yet understand why children who are involved in creative work seem to develop academically as a spin-off. But if it is true that they do, then art's place on the school timetable would seem to be influential, if not indispensable.

Art and the Individual

Education has seen as one of its main functions the development of individuality through teaching each child according to his or her particular strengths, talents, or needs. An essential characteristic of creativity is that ideas are put together to produce something new to the individual. We could hazard a guess that the really great breakthroughs in discovery and invention in our time have not happened without creative thinking coming fairly high up on the list of ingredients necessary for success. It is odd then that if we value what individuals can do through creative thinking, we do not give it more specific attention in schools. The very ability which is given such low status in some classrooms is actually what is needed in order to create something new for our society. Being inventive, being what we call creative, should be a prime concern of education and the individual. No more so than in our current society, where change comes upon us so quickly that the flexibility of thought which we associate with creativity is almost a prerequisite for keeping pace.

Through art children can learn to adapt and change ideas in an imaginative way. Imagination, in the form of mental pictures and fragments of memory, is a tool whereby as individuals we enhance our experience and mentally try things out. Art encourages children to visualize in the eye of the mind whatever might be, as well as what was and is. They learn to make comparisons between what they visualize in the mind and what ends up on paper as a piece of artwork. In encouraging children to use their imagination through art, we also help them to visualize fresh ideas, which can often give them confidence to try out new things for themselves. Much of the fantasy we attach to imagination may seem to be of little practical use but it can act as a stepping-stone to the solution of everyday problems. It may be that the truly creative thinkers as children become those adults later on in life who can see positive alternatives where others fail to envisage them.

Art sessions give children the chance to allow their individuality to be expressed through tangible form. Those very qualities which make art individual are the ones which demonstrate to others that there is more than one way to interpret things. In a field where there are no 'right' answers, individuals learn that art can be a celebration of diversity, a celebration of individuality for its own sake. Teachers can do a great deal to foster this individuality by appreciating each piece of work a child does for its very uniqueness of expression. Contrast this with classrooms where the teacher always does the problem-solving by producing stereotypes to be copied (see Chapter 3). The reason for art being undervalued by these teachers may well lie in the fact that their children have never had the experience of making their own individual contributions. We can hardly value what children have never had the chance to produce. In stereotyped art, uniqueness and individuality never become serious considerations.

If we want children's art to be individual, we need hardly be surprised if sometimes we fail to understand the work they produce. Being creative, as a teacher or child, can mean being uncertain, failing, as well as evolving new and interesting viewpoints. To fail is human, but to accept failure and live with uncertainty is a hard lesson which art often helps children come to terms with through their work. In this, the teacher's attitude is crucial and demands an accepting and encouraging response to individual work rather than a critical one. Learning to value the kind of thinking which has taken effort and courage, in order to make an individual statement, is surely what in the end makes teaching art worthwhile.

Art as an Expression of Feeling

Art is often described as the subject on the timetable through which children release their feelings. There is an idea, still prevalent in some schools, that the only good reason for doing art is for children to release emotions which have become pent up through doing academic work. Art is looked on as a purgative process through which the emotions have their outlet. In fact, children can be just as pent up doing art as they can be doing basic subjects like maths or language. Many of them give an impression of having pent-up emotions when really all that has happened is that they have run out of energy to concentrate. Traditionally, mathematics and language tend to be done in the morning. It is not surprising that art is assumed to be an emotional release if it always appears to be done just when children are less able to cope with giving their best attention. That, coupled with an atmosphere of enjoyment and expression of feeling, marks it out as a strong candidate for being therapeutic. So it can be, but if it is only for the release of the emotions, then its value is associated more with psychiatry than expressive art.

Although there is little doubt that feelings can be released through art, if this were all that art could do for children then it would rightly deserve low status as a subject. Without a great deal of alternative mental activity, such as problem-solving, discriminating, or decision-making, all that children would do was unload their feelings. What they actually created would not really matter. And if emotional unloading were the sole purpose of art, then art sessions would need to be organized rather like psychotherapy, with the teacher acting as psychiatrist. Herbert Read (1943) probably knew exactly how emotional release could become some teacher's platform for defending art. He described the art teacher as being like a 'psychic midwife', a medical missionary of the mind who was ready to deliver the artistic babies produced by the class.

Art may be a therapeutic release, but it also has the function of communicating to others through its organization of form and content. As a cathartic unloading of feeling it becomes no more valuable than the worst examples of what used to be called 'Free Expression' (see Chapter 3). Art as therapy is legitimately part of the programmes in special schools and hospitals, but its place in the general school curriculum is earned in more worthwhile ways.

Critics and educationists alike have readily accepted that art is an expression of feelings rather than a release for them. The translation of inner feelings into a concrete and public form characterizes the expression of visual form. When we look at what art does for us, feeling or emotional response is essentially what makes it live and communicate its message. If works of art do not affect us in some way it is doubtful that what we are encountering is really what can be called art. The very practice of doing art in schools inevitably draws on children's feelings about themselves and allows them to use that part of themselves which can never fully be articulated through words. Indeed feelings are readily destroyed by being put into words, unless they can find expression in a poetic sense, rather than cold-blooded description.

Through art children can identify their feelings with the subject matter they choose to interpret. Each time they paint, or draw, or make something in clay, the subject becomes part of their lives through the production of what is called (Witkin, 1974) 'feeling form'. In that sense they do indeed paint out their feelings of excitement, fear, anger, or joy in what they express (Plate 3). Yet for children, and maybe for adults, being able to identify with the subject is part of their overall progress towards finding meaning in what they do. For some children, the feelings they associate with their subject are clearly profound. Like the experience many of us have when we see the greatest works of art, or listen to the finest musical performance, children can derive assurance from their best experiences in art, that life is made worthwhile and given significance. As Robert Hughes (1980) said of art,

> The purpose of art is to close the gap between you and everything that is not you and thus proceed from feeling to meaning.

Deciding on What to Value

Within minutes of walking inside school premises it is often possible to absorb and sense the way in which art is valued. Whilst the outside catchment area of a school may be drab and boring, a real contrast can be found inside. There is of course a danger that art for display in the school becomes 'window dressing' for parents and important visitors. But the character of a school is to a great extent expressed by what it puts on the walls of its building. No amount of 'window dressing' compensates for bad art teaching so to value art mainly for the contribution it makes to display alone is not a very good reason for doing it. In fact, display as a reason for doing art can easily lead to a cul-de-sac of thought which (Chapter 3) sees end-products as the only foundation of art teaching.

A lively environment for children is quite another matter. Children thrive on seeing examples of work displayed which provoke their thinking and stimulate their curiosity. If artistic learning is to happen, then making the classrooms visually stimulating is an essential thing to do. By making the classroom look interesting and alive a teacher also demonstrates involvement and commitment. We express our educational values in everything we display, from the children's work itself, right down to the presentation of everyday materials and equipment.

Whatever finds its way to the walls of the classroom is usually only a selection of what is available. So it matters much more what value teachers put on what the children do in their art sessions rather than what a few have produced for display. Emphasizing the unique and special values that are peculiar to art gives it an importance which goes a long way towards teaching children that it has worth in its own right. This is nothing to do with how frequently art appears on the timetable but with the quality of it as an experience when it does take place.

When art becomes no more than a glorified visual aid for other subjects it loses out on the very values which make it worth doing. Here we are on dangerous ground. It is in topic work, history and other social studies, that the place of art is most frequently misunderstood. To all intents and purposes, topic-related artwork ought to offer a number of opportunities for doing creative work. Making models, drawing pictures of Viking ships, for instance, or making maps all call for artistic skills. But they hardly constitute the real value of art in children's education. In topic work (which is not the same thing as working from themes), art is often used to fulfil a rather secondary and illustrative role. It is a servant to the topic or a resource for another subject. Whilst the value of this is self-evident when children appear to be using all forms of learning within one topic, if what is done merely adds weight to the information they write about, art is robbed of its unique and creative dimension. Without counter balancing by allowing topic work to aid art, instead of the other way round, a restricted and impoverished version of artistic learning easily becomes the day-to-day practice.

Now this might seem to be over-critical of much excellent learning that is possible through topics. Yet it does bear closer scrutiny because the trap it is laying is an easy one to fall into. It is very difficult to be convinced that art is not getting a fair deal when we see children industriously working away producing illustrations and models. To any outsider there seems to be plenty of art going on and enough impressive-looking examples to satisfy the need for display around a general theme. Where then is the problem? Surely art must take second place in some topics?

Of course, it sometimes does. This is not a serious problem so long as we recognize what is happening and do not misconstrue it to be the whole art education programme. As a regular servant to the topic, art makes itself a slightly worrying companion to what is factual, rather than what is imaginative or expressive.

The desire to link art with facts is a very strong one and the rationale quite clear in some teachers' minds. As one teacher puts it,

> I believe that art is valuable in that it gives a visual representation of the written work children do. It gives more meaning to the factual work and provides added interest to the topic.

It does. But making it play such a subservient role means that its creativity is swamped by factual considerations. There is nothing wrong with making any one particular subject the centre of our own teaching style, but we need to understand what each subject has to offer, so the best can be made of it. This is especially true in first schools where subject barriers are usually not clearly defined. How guilty might we feel if each subject in turn was used as a support for topic work? Would we say that we believed language was important in that it made the facts in the topic work clearer? Would we say that the reason for doing maths was to measure things in topic work? Or would we more honestly say that language and mathematics could grow out of work on the topic just as the topic might provide some imaginative starting points for art?

The problem to be resolved in doing topic work is that as children become engrossed in fact-gathering and analysis, they tend to over-emphasize this aspect to the exclusion of being creative. Who, after all, wants a new and creative shape for a Viking ship, or some creative spellings? There is almost always a huge bank-balance of facts around to be taken account of. We can, though, have creative paintings of Viking ships and a creative use of words without ignoring the fact that their shape or spelling are somewhat fixed.

The teacher who seemed so concerned with art as a way of illustrating facts also thought it could be valuable to encourage the development of physical skill. With very young children this might be true but hardly something special to art. Children learn fine motor skills even through using a knife and fork, so to applaud art as a way of learning these skills does not count for very much. Any more than the fact that children on the whole tend to enjoy art gives it greater or less value than other enjoyable activities.

Perhaps a nightmare vision of art teaching is one where art is never valued as anything but a recreation or leisure activity. Leisure is a by-product of art which can sometimes devalue it rather than act as its driving force. Schools are not leisure centres and the fact that so much art is done in people's leisure time does not necessarily divorce it from hard work. To describe art as a leisure activity is to be in ignorance of how artistic learning occurs. If we disregard learning through the senses, and allow art to become a recreation, then what passes for art in schools need hardly be taken seriously. The fact that schools have television sets and video equipment could just as easily be connected in our minds with leisure. Yet we would not point to these as having no educational value because the content of television programmes for schools is assumed to be linked with education. If teachers find they treat art merely as a leisure activity, rather than as learning which happens to be enjoyable as well, then they should look very carefully at its content to find out what is missing.

There are many instances in which the arts have rejected the concept of being a diversion rather than making a serious contribution to life. As David Best (1985) points out,

> The seriousness of the arts consists partly but significantly in the fact that what is expressed in them feeds back into life, in the insights given into the human condition and other aspects of life. When the arts lose this seriousness they atrophy.

Art educators in this century have held different views on what are the most crucial values of art. Each one of us has the right to decide for ourselves what artistic values we emphasize above all others. Learning to see, art and the individual and art as expression of feeling are the three strands of value described here. There are many others, but at the core of most theories of artistic value lies uniqueness. Herbert Read (1943) and Elliot Eisner (1972), particularly, have a high regard for the unique qualities which only art offers. They see uniqueness as a yardstick for testing the value of art.

Many teachers will sum up the value of art in terms of its promoting a child's sense of personal worth. They view art as a way in which a child can gain confidence and a sense of being wanted, or his view of the world becoming accepted. Art teaching has the characteristic of giving us a free hand in a free syllabus, the content of which is rarely mapped out in advance. By intuition and common sense we might make good judgements about those values which we see as vital. But if we are ever to teach art with any conviction and insight, then some of what is valuable in art will need our consideration, not least because our own value system conditions how we teach.

3

Producing Original Artwork

WHEN ART is well organized and well taught, children produce work which has a flair and originality about it. No two pieces of work look alike and children delight in experimenting with ideas, solving problems and making decisions about their artwork. Watch any group of children who are totally absorbed in their painting. When they are really engrossed they show a willingness to create something which is often new and individual. To the onlooker they seem to be living in a world dictated by themselves in terms of colour, shape and line depicting their experiences. Their work has life to it and tells us things about them which we could never understand merely through words.

There are times when children are self-motivated to work but, more usually, sensitive teaching is needed to get the very best artwork even with the youngest of children. For teachers who do not think of themselves as specialists the everyday planning of creative activities for young children can be problematic. They may lack confidence in their own abilities and feel anxious about doing art alongside other areas of the curriculum. Most likely, children will use a separate part of the school for music or physical education but art will have to be fitted in wherever it can be organized within the classroom. Not only that but a teacher will need to be inventive to devise interesting art projects. There are very few useful textbooks and magazine articles in comparison with language learning or mathematics.

A common difficulty is one of persuading children they can draw. Taken together with the recurring task of devising creative projects of value, it may well seem as if other areas of the curriculum are by comparison a good deal easier to manage.

There are solutions to these problems. Producing original artwork is both rewarding and stimulating to do, largely because we can make use of children's uninhibited flair for the original. Before examining useful approaches to art teaching though, we need to look at three apparent solutions, which really do not help matters at all. They are unfortunate, though sometimes popular strategies, which need to be understood in order to avoid confusion. It would be easy enough to criticize these three by declaring them the province of the lazy or uncaring teacher. But that will not do. We need to see why they persist and what their attraction is. Why do they appear solutions, yet in reality are rather limited ways of working?

The first of these solutions is to send children away into an available part of the classroom to paint or draw unaided. They do whatever they like. Sometimes this is misnamed 'Free Expression' even though in the end it is neither very free nor is it particularly expressive. When this is done, art is sometimes regarded by the teacher as being too spontaneous to need teaching. All that seems necessary is to provide the materials, invite the children to start, and stand well clear.

Many headteachers, with good experience of the disasters which can happen to children who are left to their own devices, are eager to criticize 'Free Expression'. This probably has its roots in a time when unfettered experience of art and its materials was the fashion in schools. It was as if the children were too artistically angelic to be influenced at all by their teacher. The experience they were having was considered enough in itself.

Few teachers would disagree that at the pre-school and infant stages children need to explore new materials for themselves. Their spontaneous language of pictorial symbols expresses their experience long before they are able to write things down. In fact teachers are much more likely at this stage to play an enabling role, rather than formally teach art. They will know that the youngest of children usually need to explore over and over again what for them are new materials. But teachers will still need to support, stimulate and encourage their pupils in what they do. It is some time before any skill with the materials they try out is developed by children, and to repeat their experience with a particular medium is an important part of their early development.

What then of older infants? Can they simply carry on with the teacher leaving them to it? Quite a number of teachers are adamant about their non-intervention in art. They believe that the child's art is sacrosanct and an end in itself. After all, if the adult artist views art as a rather personal matter, then why should this not be the same for a child? They see their role as to provide materials, set the scene and disappear. The child is expected to produce artwork automatically and any involvement by the teacher is thought of as contamination of the art process. True, the dangers of being rigid and over-directive are avoided, yet almost anything the child produces becomes acceptable as art, regardless of what it is.

How attractive this is for the teacher who believes in it. When quite mindless artwork is produced the teacher cannot be held responsible. Evaluating what has been done is not necessary and the children's development can just be left to chance, or assumed to be taking place. The quality of the work does not matter either, because there were never any established aims for what was attempted by the children.

Only the most creative pupils manage to survive this for long. Other children regularly become bored when they are left to do what they like and some are greatly relieved when they are allowed to stop working. Having lost faith in their work they are bewildered by the teacher's encouragement of their efforts and begin to associate this freedom with dissatisfaction rather than enjoyment (Field, 1970). Privately they often feel angry with themselves and frustrated by not being able to think of more to do to their paintings. Subsequently, many of them lose confidence and repeat the same images over and over again, instead of trying anything new.

In other areas of the curriculum we would not give out books and expect that children would learn to read, or present practical maths equipment and expect learning to begin automatically. Yet in art sessions it is often assumed that the materials themselves will usually be enough to start children off.

It does seem that the teacher who allows this to happen displays a serious lack of responsibility. Children who are bored by their art sessions almost cry out to be given at least some small extension of their experience. And their teacher should be the one to do this if only to relate art to the rest of the curriculum. However good is the help offered by a visiting parent or classroom helper, the teacher has the ultimate responsibility for art. If this responsibility is not taken up, then it is difficult to be convinced the subject is either understood or valued as part of children's learning. More likely it has turned into a purely recreational activity through which children learn very little. They are no better or worse for the experience they have of doing art.

Left to themselves children will make marks on paper but how spontaneously and creatively they do it is questionable. Inside the classroom all too often a considerable amount of messing about with materials has been mistaken for art activity. Perhaps not so much in playgroups because it is there we can see children painting with great gusto. But when children reach school age their needs change and their artwork demands much more than encouragement from a well-intentioned adult.

We each have our own priorities for what we think is important. And opting out of any part of the school curriculum obviously leaves time for doing other things we might see as more worthwhile. For some teachers there is apparently a very clear division between what they see as being work, and art. Their priorities dictate that it is only when children have finished work that they can do art. Which is to suggest that little actual learning takes place when children are engaged in using materials like paint and crayons rather than workcards and exercise books. If art is looked on by the teacher as being other than another kind of work, in turn this is transmitted to the children. They most likely grow to see it as a not very serious activity, one similar to being let out to play.

The other two solutions taken up concern teacher-directed approaches which are at the opposite extreme from the rather *laissez-faire* nature of 'Free Expression'. Teacher-directed art is any art that is controlled by the adult in such a way that the end-product is predetermined.

This is often in evidence when teachers provide children with a ready-made kit of parts for them to assemble into a final product. Educational suppliers' catalogues show commercially produced versions which may be anything from sticky paper shapes to quite complex craft kits. Colour photographs display the finished product and associated kit of parts to make the difficult look easy. Clean children are photographed in a clean room doing clean work. The various art and craft kits produced commercially are not a serious threat to artistic development largely because of their cost. Few children ever use them for long enough because they cannot be afforded in quantity. Some specialist kits even come into the category of a headteacher's executive toy rather than an educational kit. Most of them have a certain novelty interest and a take-home product at the end.

More difficult to justify are the art kits which teachers collect together themselves for the children to assemble. Actually making these kits for children takes a lot of time and effort on the part of the teacher and any helpers. It really is hard work. But the resulting artwork is so stereotyped and identical that there is very little which could be called original about it. An example would be a kit designed by an adult from which the children made a clown puppet in order to 'develop their skills in handling materials'. All the parts would be the same. A paper cone or toilet roll for the body, card shapes duplicated with outlines, paper spots for eyes, a piece of cork for a nose and wool for the hair. The teacher might begin by showing a finished example she has made to motivate the children. They follow a step-by-step sequence of instructions and at the end of the day all the clowns look very similar to each other.

What the children produce by this method is generally less skilful than the teacher's example. Such rigid conditions have been set up that there are very few decisions the children can take about their puppets. The design is an adult one, not a child's, and such changes as there are to the facial expression or colour of the clown hardly make it original 'Child Art'.

What a lost opportunity this is. Most of the possible problem-solving is being done for the children as if they were incapable themselves. Some of them will be quite disappointed with their puppets as they compare them with the best examples they can see. Others will have been given so much help that they hardly need have been there in the first place. They are the ones who go home with what amounts to a free gift from their teacher.

There is a lot of pressure on teachers to do this instead of letting children produce art for themselves. It is particularly strong in schools where 'Child Art' is not really very well understood or highly valued.

> I very often feel under pressure from the head and parents to help children by doing work for them. When I put up a display I can see parents don't understand Child Art. But they do understand adult art. I had a parent came into school today and outside the classroom were clowns drawn by another teacher and coloured by her children. I'm sure she thought her child had done the drawing as well. Even other teachers are condescending about Child Art and spend hours working themselves into the ground doing friezes for the walls. When they see what my children do, they seem to think it is because I can't draw. I feel I have to defend what the children do by themselves because it doesn't fit in with the rest of the artwork in the school.
>
> (Teacher)

To produce work which looks just like its neighbour confirms children in the belief that there is a right way to do art. This often rests on the experience they have of seeing teachers do things for them and of copying examples they are given. When we consider that there are already many instances when children are shown 'right' ways, for example, to form letter shapes, do sums, or use practical apparatus, this is not a surprising reaction. The expectation that they will be shown how to do art the right way is hardly a shock to the system. It fits in well with a variety of things teachers already do. By controlling a step-by-step procedure to produce art, a teacher does nothing children would find revolutionary. But in the end almost all the invention and creativity is taken out of their work.

Although kits the teacher designs for children rarely leave much room for change they can nearly always be made much more creative than they are. It is difficult to believe that at Christmas time the many models of Father Christmas made from toilet rolls and cotton wool need all look so similar. In one art session a far greater range of materials can be used with very little more preparation on the teacher's part. Cotton wool is not the only material for white beards. Why, for instance, should all the models be the same size? Could a choice be given? There are a variety of ways of decorating even the most similar of Christmas shapes with different paper or fabric belts, buckles, buttons and boots. Assembling a kit in only one way is not a very worthwhile use of children's time. There are better things to do and more creative ways to do them.

The third solution is one arrived at to overcome the challenge of teaching children to draw. Substitutes for drawing, like templates or teacher-drawn outlines, are imposed in order to 'make the work look better'. If templates are used, so goes the argument, children can achieve success in producing their work. They are unable to draw things too small to be filled in with colour, and they take much longer to finish so there are fewer problems about not having plenty to do. If they are left to draw for themselves they become frustrated and do not bother to take care with what they are doing.

> My children get very disruptive sometimes if they can't draw and then art becomes a real chore. If I'm trying to cope with thirty children I can't spend time helping them to draw. When I draw big outlines for them first, the children work very well for me and do some impressive work.
>
> (Teacher)

The temptation to give out a template around which a child draws or to draw for children seems irresistible. Many children enjoy filling in outlines with colour and some will do this all day if they are allowed. When children are drawing round outlines and filling in they are certainly less demanding to teach, and we could even be convinced the artwork was the children's if it was they who actually made the marks. But at the heart of the practice is a desire to produce an image which has an adult sophistication. It is hard to understand quite what a child derives from drawing round, say, a three-quarter view of an elephant, but it is done in some classrooms. Privately we might frown at ourselves for doing the drawing for children, but publicly will we pin the work to the wall?

Taken to its logical conclusion we could imagine the aspiring art student years later attending his first life-drawing class at art school. 'Where's the template?' he asks as he has never drawn with anything else. Of course he would not be let anywhere near his art school had he not shown ability. But did the drawing skill emerge as if by chance? At the very least he must have demonstrated his talent to be given a chance to study. We all know how unskilled adults can feel about their own drawing ability. With embarrassed pride they will often claim not to be able to draw a straight line (or add up fractions, or knock a nail in the wall, or to be much more than tone deaf). But such drawing ability as there is was never developed by using a template or having the outlines drawn by anyone else. We learn things like drawing by doing it ourselves and templates ultimately have nothing to do with it. Teachers who use such devices are probably not so much concerned with drawing as with coping with the difficulties of surviving the school day. Templates are a way of keeping children busy without actually having to grasp the nettle of teaching them art.

Any teacher who is stuck with these particular substitutes for drawing has not really considered how children learn. If it is true that whenever they draw they are assimilating their experience by reconstructing it, then that reconstruction is remarkably different from the way an adult interprets things. Look at the drawing which is illustrated in Figure 5. It is something of a puzzle. To many adults it looks like a fish with fins and a tail. The 5 year-old has decorated it with lines and spots like the patterns seen on fishes. Yet what the child drew was his experience of seeing his teacher play the guitar. The guitar moved about as she played so we see a variety of positions for the neck of the instrument and more than one set of strings. There are obvious confusions about the strings and metal frets. In conversation with him, however, it turned out that the part that really interested him was doing all the spots. They were not decoration at all, but represented the places his teacher put her fingertips to make the notes. Part of the drawing at the bottom shows the hole in the main body of the guitar.

Figure 5   Age 5. 450 x 340 mm

As adults we have to adjust to a different kind of interpretation which does not follow the silhouette outline we expect to see. Had a template been used or the teacher drawn the guitar, then that boy's individual experience would never have been reconstructed as he knew it. To impose an adult concept of drawing would have been to hold back his development because an adult's drawing would have as little relation to his experience as his drawing does to ours. More than this, to set up adult standards as the ones to follow is grossly to undervalue what children can do. It is inevitable that in comparison with adults' drawings those done by children will look primitive. They need to be judged alongside development in mathematics or language and if genuinely a child's will be equally childlike.

Finding a Balance

So far, ways of coping have been mentioned which are thought to be unhelpful. In writing about the use of templates it is worth pointing out that there are still creative uses to which they can be put. Not all descriptions of these apparent solutions need be so negative. Geometric shapes can be drawn round as a basis for patternwork, and some of the older children may be able to cut out their own templates for repeating shapes. Provided that the outcome of the art is not adult and predetermined, templates have their uses. Outlines and templates for work in maths are commonly used as well and here they are appropriate to the learning which is going on. In art, colouring books, which are the most prevalent form of predetermined art, can of course be made creative if children change what is drawn already. But to pursue this when there are better ways for children to learn through art would be neither profitable nor particularly appropriate in schools. There are some colouring books which offer choice of shape, but these are the exception. Even creative use of these colouring books is best left to a wet afternoon at home.

Predetermined, teacher-directed ways of working can have the effect of undermining children's self-confidence and independence of thought. Instead of becoming used to making their own artistic decisions, the security they derive is gained from 'getting things right in the teacher's eyes'. They become dependent, rewarding to teach maybe, but miss out on the very individuality which creative work is meant to encourage. They are being mechanical, doing without thinking, and learning that art can be wrong and right.

It is not easy to find a good balance between over-directing children's art and simply leaving them to do as they please. There are many teachers who have tried to avoid structuring art and found out later that their children needed much clearer guidelines. Having endured the experience of seeing children mess about with art materials they quickly imposed a rigid style of working as an antidote. Teacher-directed work may be bad for children but many teachers have preferred it to having their art sessions get out of hand. If the extremes are to be avoided then we must look for structures which are not inflexible but at the same time practical enough to work well in the classroom.

A first step towards this is to consider and reassess how art activities are planned in the first place. Very often what happens is that we decide what the end-product will be and set about devising the means to produce it. A not unreasonable way of doing things we might think. We decide, for instance, the children will paint a picture of 'Our Street' and we see in our mind's eye what it will look like. Then we sort out the materials necessary to start. The children are given a good idea of what things they might see in the street and how they might paint them, then off they go. Or we see a piece of artwork made with tissue paper and foil perhaps, collaged and well displayed. We like the effect of it so want to try it out with our own class. Each time the procedure we adopt is the same. Think of the end-product and work backwards to the beginning to find out how to make it possible for children to do.

Without seeing examples of artwork done by other people we would never tune in to what children are capable of. But in reality the creative process (and the learning experience) lies in the gap which exists between the glimmer of an idea and its final tangible product. Creativity, it could be said, lies in the gap between intention and outcome, means and not just ends.

One of the best ways of reinforcing this is to say that *the more clearly defined the end product is* in our minds before we start, *the less creative it is likely to be* in the end.

Now this does not suit teaching very well. After all, teachers need to be clear about their ideas and transmit enthusiasm to children so that they feel able to cope. There is nearly always an end-product produced as the result of any creative work which is going on. In fact the end-product, to a certain extent, is what identifies the creative process which has taken place (see Best, 1985). Defined end-products are attractive because we know exactly what to prepare and what we are all supposed to be doing. Being vague and indecisive is no virtue. It smacks of impractical theory which has no place in the classroom. There are constraints like the rationing of materials, organization of time and distribution of workspace to consider. A clearly envisaged end-product can actually appear to be the most promising line of approach for us to think about.

Since we are surrounded by so many end-products it is not surprising they have such a hold over our thinking. Well before they reach school age, children encounter all sorts of products such as toys, furniture, houses and their own playthings. Even in their early scribbles they begin to learn that there is a connection between action and the end-product. Wooden building bricks, Lego and cardboard boxes link 'making' with 'made' and support the child's view of how he thinks the world exists (Feldman, 1982). As adults we also experience seeing end-products as the aim of a variety of occupations. The technical wizardry is much less apparent than the product which has evolved as a result of it. And even in the world of art it is the end-product which dominates the galleries of the world.

Children become conditioned from a very early age to expect to take home from playschool some artistic end-product. And with help from parents the emphasis on valuing end-products has begun. To abandon the artistic take-away in playgroups would require exceptional courage. Letting children have artwork to take home is often proof that they in fact did something with their play. In providing for end-products at the play-school stage, a habit is formed which need not necessarily spill over into infant schools, but often it does. Many children already come to their first art sessions at school to find that their experience of playschool art is largely reinforced.

No wonder there is so much resistance to art being seen as a language of expression. When there is a clear end-product in mind it is easier to see our way. There is always something to make. We can even consider the skills that are necessary to make things an end in themselves and point to folding, sticking and colouring-in as achievements in their own right. When we plan art activities solely with the end-product in mind, children can make things endlessly without our needing to consider why. Art as a language of expression on the other hand may well be a fine description of how we might see art. But has it anything to offer for the day-to-day business of planning purposeful learning?

In fact art as a 'language of expression' generally finds its way into the descriptions used by art educators to encompass a variety of desirable qualities. Feeling, expression, communication, and more obviously colour, form, line, texture, tone and pattern are associated with it, much in the same way that sound qualities are part of music. Essentially, art as a language describes the way we express our relation to the world through visual means rather than words.

How this is linked to practical planning of art activity lies in the way it can be brought into operation long before any organizational details determine what will happen. We examine first the qualities we think are important ingredients for the art session.

This can more easily be understood by taking an example found in industrial design. Supposing we were working as the designer of a new racing car. We might have *speed* in mind as an essential quality we needed. *Speed* could not be found anywhere in the component parts of the car or in its final appearance as an end-product. *Speed* is associated with what we expect the car will do.

If the truly creative part of artistic growth does not lie only in making end-products, then we must look at what children *do*, as well as what they have *made*. If we cannot be entirely certain about what they are to produce as an end-product (and of course we must have a rough idea), then we will need to give very clear guidance about what they are asked to do. Though there will be a 'mental sketch' held in our heads as to what the likely end-product will be, by concentrating on the process, individuality can become a vital ingredient, conformity the exception.

This might in some instances be as simple as getting children to decide what shape to draw, finding out how to solve a problem, or trying out three different ways of doing the same thing. Instead of being dogmatic about the final picture we wanted for 'Our Street', we would be asking them to make choices about the way they went about it. There would be the chance for more interpretation and they could arrive at a variety of end-products, not one. The children would, for example, examine the difference between one kind of window and another, one chimney and another, and build up their own detailed mental images of how they see things in terms of shapes and colours. They would be encouraged to make changes as the design progressed and extend their awareness of shape and colour through the individual decisions they made. Windows and doors would be their own windows and doors, special and personal to them rather than determined for them by an adult.

For the teacher it is not so much end-products which must be emphasized as the *process* which will lead children to produce original work. Besides asking 'What can they put in a picture of their own street?', we need to ask ourselves,

> 'How can they develop their expression through art?' (By being introduced to the variety of shapes of windows, doors, and the brickwork around them?)
>
> 'How can they become more aware of their surroundings?' (Encourage them to look, compare and collect examples, pictures, photographs?)
>
> 'How can I develop their confidence to experiment?' (By rewarding and encouraging different and original solutions to problems?)
>
> 'How can they use their feelings in what they do?' (Through drama, stories, music, and discussion?)

And more specifically,

> 'How can I get them thinking carefully about shape and pattern?'
> 'How can I develop their skills in colour-mixing?'
> 'How can they develop their drawings?'

Such questions (which here are limited to only a few) are ones which directly influence what we ask children to do. Within one piece of artwork they may be asked to think of several things even if they are very young and inexperienced artists. To help them, rough preliminary drawings might be suitable as a way of beginning, or comparison of photographs of buildings could be another stimulus to their thinking. The planning to make this possible does not happen by chance but is carefully structured to allow for as much flexibility as possible in the final results.

When children are dealing with artistic ideas, standards of achievement cannot be pointed to in the same way as with folding, sticking, filling in neatly, or using a brush. These are basic skills which may or may not lead to invention, feeling, expression and imagination, all qualities children can display through their artwork. When we consider what children will do and how their minds are occupied, we deal with important bricks from which to build up artistic learning.

One reason why being clear about the process is important is that it is much more likely to make the climate of the classroom one of thought as well as activity. Compare this with planning which is based on end-products only. If children are not really thinking about their own original artwork they are more inclined to follow the teacher's planned formula. Yet as simple a strategy as asking them to make three or four decisions themselves about their artwork avoids the predetermined, end-product thought-trap. How this is organized is the subject of the chapters which follow. There are promising opportunities for bringing variety into the process and accepting many interpretations of what is asked of children in the production of art. They will then have taken responsibility for themselves. For them the aims can be several, the choices many and the results quite individual.

4

How Children Draw

IT IS very tempting to show children how to draw. Often what happens is that a method or stereotype is taught and the children copy it. There are plenty of well-known stereotypes to be found. The zig-zag shape of a Christmas tree so frequently found in classrooms is surely more to do with adult concepts of a tree than what a child would draw. Yet many of these stereotypes are shown with the best of intentions. Children see how to draw birds by joining up two circles, or fishes by adding to an oval shape. Or they learn to draw a shape for themselves and repeat it over and over again. When they develop their own repeated symbols this is quite natural to them and part of their evolving perception (see Lowenfeld, 1970). But when shapes are forced on them by an adult, then progress may be somewhat held back.

Around the age of 7, or even earlier, children can become dissatisfied with the symbolic drawings which they have done and are likely to say that they cannot draw properly. Perhaps they pick this up from adults or they simply develop a fear of drawing something they find complicated. Very rarely do they say this when they are pattern making, printing, or drawing abstract shapes. More usually the response 'I can't draw' arises from trying to draw animals or the human figure. There are well-known difficulties like trying to draw someone's nose or a person sitting cross-legged. But apart from these especially difficult problems most children are capable of making a very good attempt to draw what they can see or imagine.

The difficulty a teacher has in persuading children to draw can partly be solved by understanding what they are capable of doing. The heart of the problem, though, lies in finding ways in which children can even begin to draw what they obviously find difficult. What do children think about when they try out the first marks on paper? What exactly does a teacher need to bring to their attention? Fundamental to teaching young children to draw are

(1) looking at pattern

(2) looking at shape

(3) practice in drawing patterns and shapes

(4) acceptance and encouragement by the teacher

(5) refusing to draw for children.

For those children who find drawing is a problem, pattern proves to be a good starting place. The search for pattern can begin with flat surfaces where the problems of drawing a three-dimensional world on two-dimensional paper are lessened. This is not a method of teaching drawing, but a good way to begin looking because what is being drawn can be thought about in simple stages. A child who cannot draw a cat, for example, can often draw a pattern of the markings on a cat's fur. Decisions about stripes, lines, or other patterns can be tackled without the complication of an outline. Inevitably, working on the pattern associated with cat fur involves looking more closely than usual at a cat or pictures of cats. From there it is a much smaller step to look more closely at the shape the cat might be. Drawing a pattern may also provide just the necessary incentive to make an extra effort to look for a shape to put it in. From observation of cat fur patterns grows the intense looking and trial and error needed to determine the cat's shape.

Similarly, a class might start out by looking at the patterns to be found on tree bark. Classroom collections of pattern, rubbings from bark and drawings of pattern might be made. All these create such an interest in looking and finding out which patterns came from which trees, that it is almost impossible not to discover something about the shape of trees at the same time. The one activity has a natural relationship to the other. Wax crayon rubbings or drawings which show changes of pattern on bark can be cut into shapes to define an outline. The simplest of collections can provide material for discussion and comparison of shape.

The way we can learn to draw shapes by making comparisons is intriguing. Our brains already have the capacity for comparing shapes and this is a sufficiently sophisticated skill to enable us to recognize people we know. We compare what we see with previously known facial measurements and their relationships, which our brain has memorized. Such comparisons with known shapes are also used when we try to draw. We compare with the known and more consciously analyse what we see in order to translate our vision to paper. With young children the process can be turned into a shape game, which includes

(1) looking for circles
(2) looking for squares
(3) looking for anything which is almost straight
(4) comparing curves and straights with each other
(5) looking for shapes which change when they are moved, or when we see them from a different angle
(6) looking for sharply defined edges, or pointed, spiked shapes.

Deciding what shape things are is usually a process of comparing with the extremes, such as straight against circle, curve against straight, or curve in comparison with a circle. A curved shape can sometimes be analysed by asking to what extent it is similar to, or different from, a circle or a straight line. We can ask what the straightest part of the curve is. What is the most curved? Which is the longest? Which the shortest? These are questions which help us to define what we are looking at by inviting judgements about similarities and differences. When children are working from memory, the process is a similar one but requires questions which trigger previous memories of particular shapes. An example of these kinds of questions comes from a game of the five-minute sort where children are not given any answers but made to visualize for themselves. The aim is to build up a strong mental image, sometimes supported by a further search for reference material, such as pictures, photographs and videotapes.

Cat and Mouse

CAT   Is its head bigger or smaller than its body?
Can you imagine it with its back arched?
Can you show me the shape in the air with your finger?
Has it got its claws out?
Is it sitting down? Stretching? Standing? What do you think it's doing?

Where does it put its tail?
What kind of tail is it?
Is it angry or friendly?
How do you know?
What markings has it on its fur?

MOUSE   Do you think it has a round nose? A pointed nose? A flat
nose? Turned up?
How long is its tail?
Is its body bigger at the back or in the middle?
Where do its whiskers go?
Has it got toes?
Are they like yours? What are they like?

The most professional of book illustrators use reference material such as photographs for their drawings, and to expect children to draw without looking at some reference is to ask a lot of them. They find animals difficult to draw in any case, especially if they are unfamiliar with them. At the stage where 5 year-olds draw a cat much as they would a human being the problem does not arise. They use a symbol for a cat and typically give it a human face. Older children draw in a more visually realistic way and need to develop their skills in observation and translate these on to paper. Each time they make comparisons of shape they develop their drawing skill a fraction more. We can think of this process as one where the act of drawing creates the need to have another look and make comparisons. In turn, looking leads to another drawing, which again promotes further observation.

Anyone who can draw a cat from memory has usually studied its shape very carefully. The drawing is done from a 'mental vocabulary' of the experience of seeing cat shapes. Each time children practise looking and drawing they add to the mental vocabulary they have acquired through the process. Their development, like that of a musician who practises music, can only take place through continual exposure to looking and drawing, comparing, contrasting, making marks and responding to them. In the end the only 'right' shapes to draw are the ones the children have found for themselves.

If we want children to progress, then attempts to tidy up drawings or draw for them are not helpful. They are counter-productive. Acceptance of children's most primitive attempts to draw is very important because without acceptance they will probably give up. It takes considerable mental effort for them to produce a drawing, and by not valuing what they do, we inevitably erode their motivation.

If we as teachers find children's efforts embarrassingly bad we are defining our own problem not theirs. They will not progress by having us force on them an adult concept of shape or pattern because at the primitive early stages of drawing they need to work through one drawing problem to arrive at another. If they are allowed to use one drawing rather like a stepping-stone to another, they will usually learn far more quickly than when an adult interferes.

When children have done their best and faced up to the difficulties of asking themselves what shape they think things are, we have little right to be dissatisfied with the results. Such drawings are not necessarily good by our adult standards but can be excellent expressions of the way children think.

Examples from Teachers

Examining what teachers say about drawing can reveal a variety of commonly experienced problems and a few useful solutions.

> Some children come to me having been to playschool, some straight from home, and they are all enthusiastic about exploring with art materials. At the age of 5 they don't have inhibitions about using paint but some do about drawing. If a child says 'Can you draw this for me?' I always get them to look and talk about it. This week we're looking at the shape of fruit and vegetables so I've set up a display in my classroom. They can touch, smell, and look at them. Today each child had to make comparisons between various shapes. An apple was like a football shape and we compared the curve of a banana with the edge of a reading book. We sorted the fruit and vegetables into sizes and we discussed how apples grew attached by the stalk. Later I had them making fruit shapes out of Plasticine so they could keep changing the shape.
>
> (Teacher of 5 year-olds)

> The 'I can't draw' response usually happens when children are trying to achieve a realistic likeness (of an animal, for instance). My own reaction is one of sympathy — I was virtually thrown out of the art class at the age of 13 because I could never do it and I had the feeling of failure. But I don't give help to any child in the form of doing the drawing. Instead, I ask the child to explain the problem — is it part of a figure he cannot do? Or has he no idea where to start? I get him to close his eyes and try to see the shape and size and pattern. I might also ask him how it feels — soft, furry,

spiky ... I also ask other children and between us we build up a picture of what it looks like. I let them look at books but not just to copy.

(Teacher of 7 to 8 year-olds)

All that happens if you show them how to draw is that they repeat your stereotype. If they copy from books or trace them they get stuck and don't seem to progress. It's like a formula which they go on repeating. So we spend a lot of time looking and comparing one shape with another.

(Teacher of 6 year-olds)

I play a classroom game where we all look at the same object to see how many different things we can see and compare.

(Teacher of 8 year-olds)

When they're looking I get them to simplify things by cutting paper shapes in black paper. It's not easy but it makes them think about shape.

(Teacher of 9 year-olds)

I get them to look at a bicycle which I prop up against a window. It's such a flat shape against the window in the classroom that it is almost two-dimensional. The children can draw it and build up their own confidence by finding they know a lot about it already, and a lot more than they thought they did.

(Teacher of 9 year-olds)

We can assess children's drawings by seeing them as an interpretation of what they themselves have experienced. In the end, we may criticize pupils for not looking hard enough but clearly we cannot criticize them for being at their particular stage of development.

Children enjoy drawing things which they are attached to or like very much. A group of children who bring in something from home, a toy or a teddy bear, will generally make a good job of drawing it because they know it so well. A familiar toy has its shape well and truly embedded in a child's consciousness and proves to be a very productive way to encourage careful observation. They can find out which is the fattest part of the toy, which the thinnest, and the act of bringing in a toy to draw also gives endless opportunities for discussion and work in other areas of the curriculum.

With most drawing problems, solutions lie in reconsidering the appearance of the object being drawn, rather than giving attention to the shortcomings of the drawing. When children are drawing something, especially something unfamiliar, the teacher's role is to talk more about the object they are drawing than the drawing itself. The importance of this teaching point cannot be emphasized too strongly. Another careful look at the source of reference for the drawing will bring about new decisions for whatever the child feels is not going well. Changes we might suggest to be made to their drawing, rather than to their observation, are often counter-productive. They are simply our own imagery. After all, which one of us has the right to impose our own literal vision on children's imaginative eyes?

Children's Imagery

Much as we might like to think that children move clearly from one stage of drawing to another, their progress is not so smooth. We cannot say that drawings are always typical of a particular age-range. Yet some understanding of what is going on is essential if we are to know what can be expected. Elsewhere (Kellogg, 1969; Gardner, 1980) much has been written about the stages children go through from scribble through symbolism and schema to visual realism. Although children usually follow these stages, they also defy the rules and produce combinations of

Figure 6   I Stayed at School All Day. Age 5. 365 x 250 mm

Figure 7 House Stereotype. Age 6. 340 x 290 mm

stages. The 5 year-old who drew the picture shown in Figure 6 used a combination of symbolic and realistic drawing. The drawing of himself is typical for a 5 year-old but the drawing of the school is not. He has looked carefully at the number of chimneys and windows. The windows are not simply placed at each corner (see Figure 7) but are set in from the edge of the brickwork as they would be in reality. Why then is there a mixture of styles?

A useful way to interpret the two styles is to think of how children reconstruct their experiences. At the moment of drawing, this particular child (who lived close to the school) looked at the school buildings and drew what he could see. He counted the chimneys and windows and kept looking at the school from outside. When he put himself in the picture he was certainly not working from a full-length mirror, and reconstructed his knowledge of himself by producing a symbol as large as the school. He still drew himself the largest because at this stage he considers he is the most important feature of the drawing. Yet he does not worry at all about combining inner thoughts and outer vision in the one piece of work. The

Figure 8   Houseface. Age 5. 295 x 210 mm

distinctions an adult might make are not there. Even houses and people can become fused together in a child's mind as a drawing begins as one thing and ends up looking like another (Figure 8).

Typically, what can be expected from 2 to 4 year-olds is scribble. Scribble is to drawing what babbling is to talk. From rather random marks they make when they first are given paper and crayons, children develop enough control to make the scribble more ordered and intentional. They like scribbling and will repeat the activity just for the fun of it. Occasionally within their scribbles they will find images by accident such as boats, people, houses and themselves. If asked, they will invent subject matter for the pictures even when none existed. Parents often ask what things have been drawn and their children become very practised at giving answers, even if they have to invent these.

Their first really recognizable and intentionally drawn shapes are circles or oval shapes. Before long these become 'Me', 'My Mum' or 'My Dad'. As we can see from the example in Figure 12, a pre-school child will sometimes add expression to the face. The most important symbols are nearly always the largest, often representing the child himself, and there is no sense of perspective or space as we know it. When such drawings are produced it is not uncommon to find children returning to scribble within a few seconds of concentrated drawing. They still enjoy scribbling, even though they can draw symbols, and are reluctant to give it up. Art materials are as yet fairly new to children of this age and playing with them is just as important as doing any drawing. At school the scribbling is still there (Figure 13). Houses are drawn but scribble is still included.

Figures 9, 10 Scribble. Age 3. 290 x 420 mm

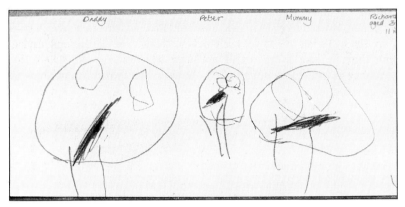

Figure 11   Daddy, Peter, Mum. Age 3. 350 x 150 mm

In the symbolic drawings of people, a private code is used and we more or less have to read the image as if it were a word. Symbols for people are drawn almost looking like tadpoles. They have no neck, sometimes no body, arms, fingers, or toes. Quite what meaning can be attached to this kind of drawing is uncertain. It is a very dangerous practice to read too much into children's drawings and we are very often misled. We can say that these drawings describe more how they think of themselves than

Figure 12   Daddy with a Big Face. Age 4. 580 x 350 mm

Figure 13 Hills and Scribble. Age 5. 450 x 320 mm

what they actually see when they look. They are not very aware of their own neck and their head feels big in comparison with the rest of their bodies. They cannot see their shoulders, so the way they draw turns out to be a satisfactory description of how they feel they are, rather than a very recognizable likeness.

When children draw from experience of looking, they often draw expressive essentials which adults miss. The character of a spider (Figure 14) is shown as something moving with lots of legs and drawn larger than life. Mother is recovering, tea in hand, and the scene is expressed almost like a drama. The blackbird (Figure 15) is drawn with a plump and well-fed look about it. Like the spider which moves, and the drawing of a guitar (Figure 5, in Chapter 3), there is no attempt to draw an exact perceptual illusion. The images we see are very advanced personal schema but still drawn in response to a knowledge of experiences.

From the age of around 6 to 9 years the schema change and become more elaborate. We can find drawings of girls (Figure 19) where a triangle forms the basis for the drawing, and we can see examples of the influence of other school activities on art. Often no real distinction is made between writing patterns and drawing (Figures 16 and 17). Another characteristic is 'X-ray' drawing, which we can see in the drawing of a house and garage (Figure 18) where there is no attempt to

Figure 14   Mum Frightened by a Spider. Age 5. 255 x 175 mm

Figure 15   Blackbird. Age 6. 280 x 330 mm

Figure 16 My Best Writing. Age 5. 250 x 150 mm

Figure 17 Writing/Landscape. Age 6. 305 x 180 mm

Figure 18   X-Ray House. Age 5. 310 x 240 mm

hide the car. The X-ray picture tells us what is known to be there so it follows that we can also see inside the house.

Patterns are derived from the experience of filling in mathematics worksheets and writing. Number and drawing feature together if a child decides they will.

Awareness of space is often confused in young children's minds and they may solve problems by working all round their paper (Figure 19) so we have no firm idea of where the top and bottom of the room is. We must remember that at this age to teach perspective would be inappropriate as perception of space is unlikely to be as we experience it as adults. The circular expression of a dance is that particular child's way of solving the problem of coping with drawing three-dimensional space.

The age of 8 to 12 years is dominated by a greater concern for accuracy of detail and can broadly be called a stage of visual realism. No longer do we always see people drawn with both arms in view if they are standing sideways. One arm is allowed to disappear behind a person's body. For boys particularly, this is an age when they draw subject matter like space-ships and helicopters, launches and battles. Not a detail is left to chance. There is some evidence that the organization of the design is carefully thought about, even the placing of the image on the paper is more critical than before. A whole tale can be told in some drawings where planes take off, engage an enemy, shoot, explode and dive, all within the same picture.

Such a concern is there for including detail that excellent opportunities present themselves for teachers to make use of this aspect of drawing. Older infants or primary children thrive on learning to develop detailed observation. Theirs is a world where drawing refuels their curiosity and lends itself to discovery. The stages they have been through, scribble, symbols, schema and visual realism, are each important experiences which a teacher could impede. Children must proceed at their own pace. Knowing the stages gives us the opportunity to match activities to what the children are capable of producing, and avoids forcing upon them those images for which they are not yet ready. The fixed blue line at the top of a painting and the green one at the bottom are sky and grass until the children are ready for it to be different. Faces are painted blue, green, or purple, until flesh colours seem important enough. Focusing their attention on the sky, or on flesh tones, but not demanding that sky meets

Figure 19　All Around Dance. Age 6. 195 x 143 mm

Figure 20   Space Shuttle. Age 8. 340 x 300 mm

ground, or that flesh is pink, encourages them to look and question what they see. The search must still be theirs, not ours.

Only experience gives us a true indication of what can be expected from children and without finding out for ourselves we could very easily over-direct them. The stages of development outlined here are a guide to expectations but no indication of what children can achieve for themselves. If we over-direct them or attempt to condition what they draw, we are misunderstanding the nature of art teaching and the minds of children. Then, they draw with only a fraction of their expressive power and energy. If we understand, encourage and direct their attention towards looking carefully, they draw with remarkable conviction and confidence.

5

Developing Ideas

Using Themes

New materials, fascinating though they are to children, cannot be relied on to provide an endless source of ideas. Children enjoy discovering what various media will do and such exploratory activities characterize many art sessions. Important differences between one material and another cannot be denied, but if development is to take place, simply to confront children with a change of media is not enough. The development of their artistic ideas is a worthwhile activity and should concern us more than any new material. Developing ideas is also something which occupies the teacher. A commonly experienced difficulty is that of generating interesting ideas and exciting alternatives for children to try out. There is an unwritten assumption that the teacher's responsibility is to do just this.

Developing children's ideas is also educationally profitable. The one-off art activity has its place, but can fail to make contact with any other part of the curriculum and may not even fit easily into the rest of the art programme. Changing, adapting and adding to ideas can lead children in new directions. Disparate areas of the curriculum are threaded together and children make more of the original impetus to create. There may always be good reasons for providing the isolated short activity, one unrelated to any other context (shortage of a special material would be an example, children's brief attention span another). Even so, developing ideas through the use of themes is more likely to generate enthusiastic learning. If a number of ideas do not quite constitute a theme, they can still encourage learning to take place across curricular boundaries.

The notion of development expressed here is that ideas, explored by the teacher with the children, in a sequence or progression, will have a relationship one to another. Working with the children, the teacher makes use of often unexpected contributions by linking these to ideas in the original theme. Of course, ideas and themes in themselves do not automatically suggest what opportunities for related learning will unfold. Choices have to be made and decisions taken in the light of what looks the most promising. For that reason, a theme needs to be sufficiently open to allow flexibility of purpose and the chance to cover an extensive area of interests. The popularity of themes like 'The Sea', or 'Animals', probably arises from their being sufficiently adaptable to a variety of possible outcomes. From the broadest of beginnings, material can be chosen, refined, put aside, or eliminated, as its educational potential becomes apparent.

Wordspill Themes as a Resource

A useful strategy for developing ideas is to work the way many cartoonists do when they are in search of a punchline. They spill as many words on to paper as they can in connection with the cartoon. The technique is also used on Study Skills courses. Once the paper is filled with word associations, and randomly placed ideas in connection with a theme, links can be made. Words can lead to other words, more words, reminders of any activity to be done, or new relationships between ideas. The resource is developed as a personal 'think-tank' and is quite uncon- ditionally filled with anything which is triggered by the theme. One way of producing a good idea is to have lots of ideas and associations, then pick the best. Wordspill makes this a possibility.

Suppose we pick a theme, 'Animals', and begin. By free association of words we might arrive at ANIMALS, wild, domestic, camouflage, colour. These words could become themes in themselves or short-lived ideas for art activities. They also provide the beginning of a much larger resource which could evolve over a period of days or weeks. Imagine a sheet of A3 paper pinned up in the kitchen. It begins as shown in Chart 1 and develops more fully to produce a wordspill resource as shown in Chart 2.

Chart 1   Free Association on a Theme

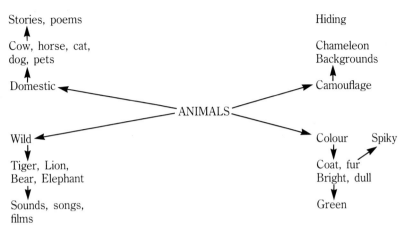

Stories, poems

Cow, horse, cat,
dog, pets

Domestic

ANIMALS

Wild

Tiger, Lion,
Bear, Elephant

Sounds, songs,
films

Hiding

Chameleon
Backgrounds

Camouflage

Colour   Spiky

Coat, fur
Bright, dull

Green

Some Useful Wordspill Themes

There is some overlap possible with themes and these should be treated
as if they were the beginning of a wordspill chart.

Reflections	Holes	Gems
Growth	Fire	Old
Space	Spring	New
Fear	Summer	Churches
Dark	Autumn	Contrast
Flight	Winter	Biological
Magic	Work	Prehistoric
Night	Surprises	Machines
Mystery	Boats	Outer Space
Parks	Cars	Monsters
Shops	Lorries	Food
Buildings	Trains	Wood
Factories	Transport	Pattern
Uniforms	Stairways	Camouflage
Police	Underground	People
Milkman	The Sea	Jungles
People Who Help	Underwater	Carnival
Time	Animals	Fair

Spirals	Insects	Fantasy
Circles	Red, Yellow, etc.	Fish
Squares	Colour	Fungi
Triangles	Texture	Butterflies
Oblongs	Lines	Moths
Rectangles	Gardens	Fables
Trees	Playtime	Ponds
Leaves	Chimneys	Plants
Bark	Doors	Wild Flowers
Hedges	Lights	Costume
Farms	Birds	Earth
Surfaces	Faces	Travel
Insides	Masks	Stars
Inside/outside	Windows	Races
Habitats	Formal	Castles
Weather	Repeating	Walls
Skies	Abstract	Fences
Water	Form	Markets
Thin	Transparent	Smooth
Miniature	Giant	Liquids
Games	Light	Surfaces
Stripes	Metals	Vegetables
Wheels	Tracks	The Planets
Units	Tangles	Stones

As with the examples in Charts 1 and 2, each theme can provide a starting point for many areas of the curriculum. The two examples given in Charts 3 and 4 are taken from the list at random. To develop these it is sometimes a good idea to draw a circle round any word in the flow chart and try making this a new theme.

Making Choices

We might think that a wordspill, like the ones shown in the charts, is enough to spark off a dozen ideas for activities. No doubt there are some teachers who find they can think of a whole variety of inspired ideas. But they still make choices and take decisions to structure and sequence activities, no matter how spontaneously they might feel they are working. These choices are common to all art activities. Decisions are taken about

Chart 2   A Wordspill Resource

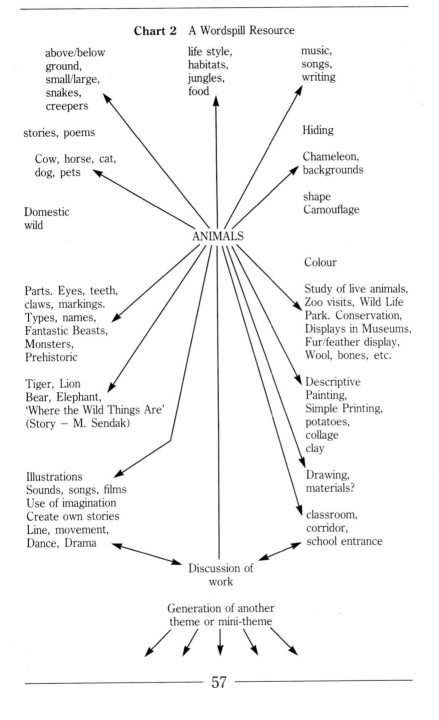

above/below
ground,
small/large,
snakes,
creepers

life style,
habitats,
jungles,
food

music,
songs,
writing

stories, poems

Hiding

Cow, horse, cat,
dog, pets

Chameleon,
backgrounds

Domestic
wild

shape
Camouflage

ANIMALS

Colour

Parts. Eyes, teeth,
claws, markings.
Types, names,
Fantastic Beasts,
Monsters,
Prehistoric

Study of live animals,
Zoo visits, Wild Life
Park. Conservation,
Displays in Museums,
Fur/feather display,
Wool, bones, etc.

Tiger, Lion
Bear, Elephant,
'Where the Wild Things Are'
(Story − M. Sendak)

Descriptive
Painting,
Simple Printing,
potatoes,
collage
clay

Illustrations
Sounds, songs, films
Use of imagination
Create own stories
Line, movement,
Dance, Drama

Drawing,
materials?

classroom,
corridor,
school entrance

Discussion of
work

Generation of another
theme or mini-theme

Chart 3 'Trees' Resource Chart

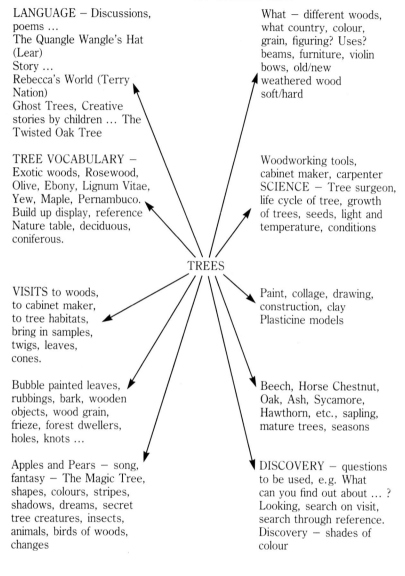

LANGUAGE − Discussions, poems ...
The Quangle Wangle's Hat (Lear)
Story ...
Rebecca's World (Terry Nation)
Ghost Trees, Creative stories by children ... The Twisted Oak Tree

TREE VOCABULARY −
Exotic woods, Rosewood, Olive, Ebony, Lignum Vitae, Yew, Maple, Pernambuco. Build up display, reference Nature table, deciduous, coniferous.

VISITS to woods,
to cabinet maker,
to tree habitats,
bring in samples,
twigs, leaves,
cones.

Bubble painted leaves, rubbings, bark, wooden objects, wood grain, frieze, forest dwellers, holes, knots ...

Apples and Pears − song, fantasy − The Magic Tree, shapes, colours, stripes, shadows, dreams, secret tree creatures, insects, animals, birds of woods, changes

What − different woods, what country, colour, grain, figuring? Uses? beams, furniture, violin bows, old/new weathered wood soft/hard

Woodworking tools, cabinet maker, carpenter
SCIENCE − Tree surgeon, life cycle of tree, growth of trees, seeds, light and temperature, conditions

TREES

Paint, collage, drawing, construction, clay Plasticine models

Beech, Horse Chestnut, Oak, Ash, Sycamore, Hawthorn, etc., sapling, mature trees, seasons

DISCOVERY − questions to be used, e.g. What can you find out about ... ? Looking, search on visit, search through reference. Discovery − shades of colour

Chart 4   'Pattern' Resource Chart

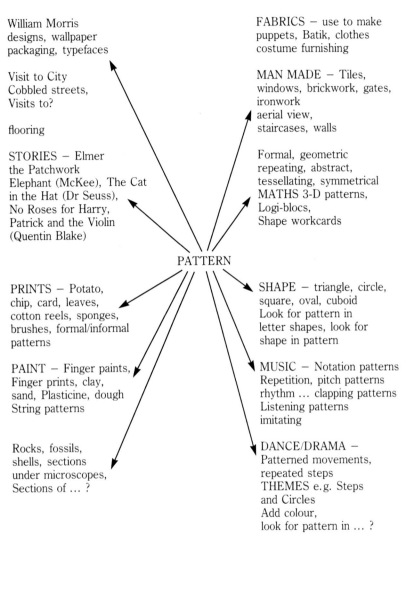

William Morris
designs, wallpaper
packaging, typefaces

Visit to City
Cobbled streets,
Visits to?

flooring

STORIES – Elmer
the Patchwork
Elephant (McKee), The Cat
in the Hat (Dr Seuss),
No Roses for Harry,
Patrick and the Violin
(Quentin Blake)

FABRICS – use to make
puppets, Batik, clothes
costume furnishing

MAN MADE – Tiles,
windows, brickwork, gates,
ironwork
aerial view,
staircases, walls

Formal, geometric
repeating, abstract,
tessellating, symmetrical
MATHS 3-D patterns,
Logi-blocs,
Shape workcards

PATTERN

PRINTS – Potato,
chip, card, leaves,
cotton reels, sponges,
brushes, formal/informal
patterns

PAINT – Finger paints,
Finger prints, clay,
sand, Plasticine, dough
String patterns

Rocks, fossils,
shells, sections
under microscopes,
Sections of ... ?

SHAPE – triangle, circle,
square, oval, cuboid
Look for pattern in
letter shapes, look for
shape in pattern

MUSIC – Notation patterns
Repetition, pitch patterns
rhythm ... clapping patterns
Listening patterns
imitating

DANCE/DRAMA –
Patterned movements,
repeated steps
THEMES e.g. Steps
and Circles
Add colour,
look for pattern in ... ?

what stimulus to provide, what materials to make available, what learning to emphasize and what problems to pose for children to think about.

There are four areas in which artwork can be stimulated. After deciding which of the four should be the starting point, teachers can quickly touch on the other three areas once work is under way. All four become integrated but initially a choice is made to stimulate a response to one of the following:

(1) Something SEEN, FELT,   (2) MEMORY OR
     HEARD, TOUCHED   IMAGINATION

(3) MATERIALS   (4) TECHNIQUE

If the wordspill for the theme 'Trees' was being used we might provide any of the stimuli shown in Chart 5. (The ideas which work the best are the ones we ourselves decide on. The chart only gives examples to illustrate each area in turn.)

Chart 5 Four Areas of Stimulus

Example Area 1	Provision of a display 'Trees' table — tree bark, twigs, photographs, visual aids, diagrams, reference books, wood samples, paper, furniture, seeds. Fruits, blossom, leaves. Discuss, sort, examine, similarities/differences, features.
Example Area 2	Imaginative stories about trees, memory, magic trees (fantasy), moving trees, golden tree. Brightly coloured imagined trees, animals, insects, tree dwellers (fantasy), forest dwellers (fantasy), e.g. 'Grumbly the Worst Wizard', poems about trees, songs, drama (fantasy), music *(No looking at all)*.
Example Area 3	Provision of collage materials, glue, scissors, paper, drawing materials, as a stimulus for discussion on trees.
Example Area 4	Demonstration of a technique for creating tree bark patterns in clay or Plasticine. (Technique demonstrated but bark pattern not used in demonstration).

Tastes vary, and whilst one teacher happily gives out a range of materials from which children choose, another may decide one material is quite enough to organize. Providing a variety of materials could mean children do not need the same kind of help at the same time. Choosing one material gives children a chance to see what others do with it. Whatever decision is taken it will influence the artwork in an important way. The questions that naturally arise are, do the children choose or does the teacher, and can this vary? Sometimes the teacher may deliberately limit materials and on other occasions the children's choice may be an important part of the activity.

Materials as commonplace as paints are so varied now that comparing the work of one class with another is revealing. The artwork may be different in ideas but is characterized by the kind of paint used, how it is mixed and what paper children paint on. In one classroom we see white paper and bright PVA paints. In another, children are mixing powder colour and painting on sugar paper. One school orders a particular red, another orders a particular green, each available paint becoming a trade mark of the children's work.

Decisions taken about stimulus and materials relate to the purpose or the learning content of an activity. Here we have the next step in a sequence of events which turn theory into practice. Of course, it may be difficult to analyse what the purpose of a session is, and a glance in some classrooms reveals how obscure purposes can be. Excellent teachers of art often have no idea how they teach and shy away from any conscious analysis of purpose in what they do. Maybe their thoughts are that there needs to be no particular emphasis or purpose to the session. They may decide that the experience of doing art is enough in itself and to include a conscious purpose is to be over-directive. This may be true for a few children, but those teachers who argue they have no need to decide on any purpose will find themselves doing so, even if it is subconsciously done. We all shape the purpose and content of sessions by what we put in and leave out. There are excellent teachers who are very conscious of their aims and objectives. Others, equally excellent, appear by intuition to give an emphasis to learning, the origins of which usually lie in their own very positive and purposeful attitudes.

Since there could be several reasons why a particular session is taking place, purpose is not confined to a single objective. But there are various aspects of artistic learning which might be included. For example, we can choose to emphasize:

(1) learning about line
(2) learning about colour
(3) learning about shape
(4) learning about pattern
(5) learning about design
(6) learning about the medium
(7) learning a particular technique
(8) learning about texture.

All these form the basis of rather formal elements of art. The purpose of our sessions is far wider and can include

(9) stimulating an imaginative response to ...
(10) encouraging colour-mixing in ...
(11) developing new skills in ...
(12) increasing awareness of ...
(13) consolidating work in ...
(14) exploring the qualities of ...
(15) expressing the movement in ...
(16) expressing feelings of ...
(17) trying out/combining ...

To give a session purpose it may be enough to discuss or bring to children's notice just one or at the most three of these learning aims. More than three ceases to be effective as a focus to the session. Deliberately choosing has the effect of strengthening the impetus of the activity and sharpening the teachers' awareness of what they are trying to encourage. Naturally much depends on how the work develops and it is not unusual to find that things can change. It would be far too rigid an approach to stick to one aim or objective come what may. The nature of art is to respond to changes that take place. The objectives of any session should never be contrived simply to reassure ourselves that we are actually teaching. Good practice usually includes taking advantage of the unexpected and learning from it. Inevitably, art is meant to develop awareness of 'something'. But to find out what that might be raises art above the superficial level of its being for entertainment or recreation.

Intuitive teachers may still find that consciously to think about purpose seems an academic nuance. They argue that it is sufficient to give children confidence or to teach them that nobody fails at art in their particular classroom. True, these are worthy aims, but the best teachers already make further demands on themselves when they exercise professional judgement. They still decide to emphasize certain skills, like development of imagination, or awareness of pattern, for example, but in a less conscious way. There is no doubt that this is possible with some experience of teaching. Yet to make a deliberate and conscious decision about purpose, if only for a day, is still educationally sound practice. Its effect on work needs to be seen and experienced before a more haphazard set of purposes is adopted.

Development without Themes

In contrast to working through themes, development is possible as children respond to what they are already doing. Quite outside any considerations of there being a theme, some visual ideas just take off as children make links with other forms of knowledge.

> We were looking at peacock feathers, some of the children using hand lenses to magnify. The purpose of it was to develop their skills in observation ... one boy noticed that the pattern on a feather is rather like an eye ... we discussed real eyes and things that looked like eyes. They looked at each other's eyes and compared shapes, lines and colours. When it came to doing some artwork, some did peacocks, some patterns based on feathers, others eyes and patterns based on eye shapes.
>
> (Primary teacher)

Once ideas like these develop to include a new subject, there are obvious opportunities for making further links with simple science, maths and language. Graphs of eye colouring within the class, stories, songs and discussion of how eyes function can prove valuable vehicles for learning. Unexpected events do not always destroy planning. On the contrary, they often enhance it.

> My children were talking about a story we were reading which was all about Dutch children enticing storks back to their village. I got them drawing imaginary characters from the story and for that they had to think their way into being part of the action. We did some role-play in drama and that led on to very simple mask-making. One girl had the idea we could draw a strip cartoon of the events in the story so we did. Then two of the boys wanted to make a shoebox 'peep' show and we enacted part of the story with them to help them get into the feel of what they wanted to include.
>
> (Primary teacher)

Dramatic play is a superbly rich way of letting children feel from within in order to develop ideas for artwork. Using drama is not everybody's strength but for some teachers artwork borders on performance as they develop ideas with their children.

> I must confess it's difficult to dramatize tree bark. If we did it in drama we'd do rough scratchy movements to try to 'feel' our way into the imagery ... tree ring movements ... they internalize what they're doing ... they experience fear, happiness, sadness ... I remember we'd been working in art on a theme of 'Empty Things', objects which contain nothing. One boy drew the outlines of a rainbow which had been a theme in drama and song. I thought 'Oh dear, he hasn't understood.' I asked him why he'd drawn a rainbow in pencil. 'Well,' he said, 'it's an empty rainbow ... no colours in it.' I thought that was very creative thinking.
>
> (Reception teacher)

Games of the Imagination

An intriguing device for developing ideas comes from Robert Eberle (1971), who in his children's book *Scamper* suggests a way of stretching the mind. The Scamper technique can be applied to drawings, session plans, writing and in fact anything which requires designing or planning. We can imagine it applied to ideas generated through themes, or we can think of it as a checklist to be used before ideas become too firmly fixed. Based on *Your Creative Power* by Alex Osborn (1948/1972), Eberle suggests:

S	SUBSTITUTE	To have a person or thing act or serve in the place of another.
C	COMBINE	To bring together or unite.
A	ADAPT	To adjust for the purpose of suiting a condition or purpose.
M	MODIFY	To alter, change the form or quality.
	MAGNIFY	To enlarge, make greater in form or quality.
	MINIFY	To make smaller, lighter, slower, less frequent.
P	PUT TO OTHER USES	To be used for purposes other than originally intended.
E	ELIMINATE	To remove, omit, or get rid of, a quality, part, or whole.
R	REVERSE	To place opposite or contrary, to turn round.
	REARRANGE	To change the order, different plan, layout, or scheme.

The Scamper technique can be used to play out five-minute games where children imagine what objects would be like bigger, smaller, combined, rearranged and so on. Or this mind-flexing idea can be applied to other areas of the curriculum so that questions arise:

S   Can you think of a new way of using this?
C   What do you think might happen if you try to put these together?
A   What else is like this?
M   Can you imagine this bigger? Smaller?
P   Do you think we might use this for ... ?
E   What might this be like if you got rid of ... ?
R   What happens if you turn it backwards ... or upside down?

Artists, writers, composers and designers exercise many of these Scamper methods quite naturally as they create. 'Scamper' encapsulate a process which is true to the artist in one particularly important respect When ideas are formulated they do not remain static and fixed for al time. The creative process is an unending, living, transforming one. Fa from acting on one idea without modification, creative thinkers tenc continually to reflect on the ideas they have evolved. They prefer to live with less certain outcomes and adapt solutions to different circumstances.

In practical terms the questions above, which as teachers we might ask of our children, are also those which apply to any planning we might do ourselves. A wordspill resource can be adapted using 'Scamper', as can the art activities which are already under way. The more varied the development of ideas, the greater is the range of options open to children from which to make choices, take decisions and think independently. No idea is ever sacrosanct and nothing is really a final statement of intent. Even the so-called 'finished' artwork can change.

> A word my children love to learn is 'embellish'. It arose because I found my children tended to rush work and finish their art very quickly without taking much trouble over it. We discussed embellishment and decoration and now they very often embellish things with pattern ... sometimes a design will go on for days as they leave it and come back to it, changing and adding to it.
>
> (Teacher of 7 year-olds)

Not content to leave ideas where they are, this teacher (see Plate 6) pushed the children further by giving a new direction to the work. In her judgement it was necessary to teach children that something else could be done. There would be other times when the best thing to do was move on to another idea entirely, because the work was complete enough in itself. For a teacher whose style was more geared to materials and techniques, work could develop in a different way.

> I know a lot grows out of the materials they use ... I give them a choice ... if they've done any simple printing with potatoes, I find they often want to print instead of draw or paint. There's quite a range of materials which they can go and get for themselves ... I often keep one or two things back, like a special paper or fur fabric, so I can introduce it later when they've got started ... but I do want them to take decisions about the materials they use ... a lot seems to come out of doing that. Sometimes they also need to see a technique demonstrated ... we were doing a topic on 'Divers under the Sea' and I decided to show them what could happen if the paper was flooded with water and colour added ... when it was dry, they added collage and paint on top ... some of them added pastel drawing as well.
>
> (Teacher of 8 year-olds)

It is quite surprising how little encouragement some children need to think creatively. If a lot of artwork takes place around them they accept it as a normal way of thinking about ideas and the process becomes self-generating. Children make relationships between one idea and the next in a far more imaginative way than do many adults. To a child, there are all sorts of fantastic possibilities, and to encourage a developing idea, often all that is necessary is for the teacher to join in the fantasy. Acceptance of children's varied and bizarre ideas persuades them to develop much more in their artwork than if they only respond to suggestions their teacher makes. Too many suggestions from the teacher can elicit over-directed work and too few can result in little extension of their thinking.

Hitting the right balance requires a degree of judgement which is only possible as we gain experience and understanding of art. But there is no doubt that holding back our own suggestions, and trying to develop those ideas which are offered, is far better than making children dependent through over-direction. Whether we avoid this through developing themes with them, playing imaginative games, questioning, or stimulating their thinking, requires judgement. Perhaps the risk worth taking in art teaching is continuously to develop children's ideas and see what results. It is far more creative a teaching strategy than identifying some tangible end-product towards which we steer the children. Developing ideas demands sensitivity and a willingness to step back more than occasionally to allow children to take the initiatives. They will develop artistically provided they are allowed to follow their ideas through by themselves. To do so they need skilful guidance, rather than rigid direction, which is why no substitute has yet been found for high-quality teachers.

6

Classroom Organization

A FEATURE of work with very young children is that they often work in groups for much of the day. Further up the age-range, formal class teaching may be more usual, with creative artwork being taught to the whole class. Whether to put children in groups or not is a matter of choice, and the outcome reflects the educational philosophy of the school or teacher. Besides this, the effect of teacher-appraisal can tempt teachers to play safe and abandon group teaching in favour of class teaching. There might be considerable educational losses to the early years age-range. Co-operative work, where there is a good exchange of language between children, could diminish. The range of activities could be severely restricted, and the scope of art teaching would be limited. This is especially true where large numbers of children are concerned.

The issue is one left open for debate. What is best is what organization is appropriate at the time, not simply what we happen to believe in, though personal teaching style naturally has an influence. There are enough opportunities for formal class teaching later on in children's lives without introducing it too soon. Teaching in the early years usually demands far more flexible ways of looking at classroom organization if the best is to be gained from it.

However brilliant the ideas for producing wonderful artwork, without a firm grasp of how organization can be effective, success is doubtful. There is little reason to think that children will work independently in art without first having learned skills and strategies necessary for coping. Of course, a price must be paid for good organization. It is demanding and even complex, especially if the school operates an integrated curriculum. Yet it is necessary because the alternatives to a well-run classroom lead to mediocre, not to say unprofessional teaching. A well-organized class commands the respect of other members of staff and is one of the indicators of an ability to manage groups, the whole class and all the hardware in terms of practical materials and equipment.

> I don't always teach groups. Sometimes I have one group and the rest of the class doing something else, sometimes I teach the whole class, other times I divide up the class into as many as four groups – it depends what we're doing.
>
> (Teacher of 6 year-olds)

> I never have all my groups doing completely different activities. There's usually something in the curriculum I want to emphasize with more than one group.
>
> (First school deputy headteacher)

Organizing Groups

Suppose the policy was to teach children in groups. There could be several ways of organizing this to the best advantage, and here we cannot limit strategies to art, because group organization obviously affects all areas of learning.

If a class is divided into groups, then to free the teacher to teach one group, it follows that the other groups must do tasks with which they are already familiar. It is surprising how many student teachers think they can deal with each group by dashing round from one to the other. In practice this is not very effective but an understandable response to a difficult problem. The results can often be to increase wear and tear on the nerves and eventually invite the possibility of becoming physically and mentally drained. A more effective strategy might be to choose one group we intend to teach art and involve the other groups in revision or practice tasks, something which they are used to doing. (In a reception class, for example, this could include structured play activities and with older children good-quality workcards, board games, patternmaking, or possibly practice in handwriting.)

Given that we cannot teach all of the children all of the time, it is only reasonable to recognize that to use these practice tasks is a somewhat imperfect solution to an intractable problem. A vital element in organizing groups, however, is delegation (see Taylor, 1971). Children need, for instance, to find their own scissors, and can do this from habit if they know where they are kept and that they are expected to do so. This is not to say they always will, but a good organizational policy is to teach as if they will for some of the time. Then they can learn to cope with simple practice tasks in a more independent way.

The quality of those tasks need not necessarily be poor, neither need they be dull or boring. But like most teaching methods where children are meant to work unaided, children's skills in working independently are only gradually built up. The less worthwhile task, which we might use with an inexperienced group, can gradually be replaced with a more demanding one as learning and resourcefulness develop.

The aim is to try to buy time for work with the teaching group. As far as the other children are concerned, the promise of better things to come is sometimes the best we can hope for. Our attention can then turn to the group which really demands it, the one we are teaching. In practice, moving quickly from group to group may appear to be effective, but we should ask what children learn from such a brief contact with us. Contact with the teaching group does not, after all, rule out work with other groups. As one teacher points out,

> When I'm teaching maths I have three groups ... a 'teaching' group, a 'revision' group and a 'practice' group. I tend to move from my teaching group to my revision group (who are usually consolidating work they started the previous day), to my practice group. Next session they change round.
>
> (Teacher)

If the teaching group is taught with future practice tasks in mind, we can more easily move on to another group and work with them. Individuals within a group never finish work at the same time, so built in to the teaching of most subjects there is a need to set further tasks which the children can do when they have completed their work. It is a pity if the extra task is always to draw a picture, though it cannot be denied this is a legitimate practice task. The trouble is that drawing a picture does not always practise what the children are being taught at that moment. Often it relies on a quite different area of thought.

A familiar trap to avoid is one of describing what we personally value in the rest of the curriculum as being *work* and anything else as *play*. How, for example, would we describe structured learning through play? Is it work? Or is it play? Why should we think of making the distinction? Is it because we want to convince children that they should endure a certain misery and difficulty in work? Or is it, perhaps, that the artwork we do is not taken seriously enough and therefore mistakenly associated with enjoyment or recreation? The point is made here because the way we view art activities clearly influences the way groups work. It would be a great pity if there were *work groups* and, in contrast, groups we described as *recreation groups* operating in the same room.

Although mathematics has been mentioned as an example of group organization, there is no reason why the same approach should not apply to art. Children need to build up independent thinking skills for considering what they do with art materials. We could have four art groups, but more likely art and language, or art and mathematics groups working. Alternatively, three or four art groups could take it in turns to work throughout the day. Whatever the style, the teaching group in art needs to be treated exactly as we would any other subject.

Variations of these combinations can be tried to find out how effectively the teaching group can be managed. Effective group management is crucial to learning, but it would be easy to confuse it with effective teaching. In many instances, the ability to manage groups has little relationship with a session's content or aims. In theory, an art group could be managed well without ever having its attention drawn to anything particularly worthwhile. In practice, it would learn little except perhaps what was picked up by chance.

When, for example, children become adept at finding pattern in everyday surroundings, this is often the result of careful work done when they were in a teaching group. In the whole class they can still learn through discussion and observation, but it is in the small group that ability can really be extended. Not only is the teaching group crucial to learning, but in art there are similarities with mathematics. We quite rightly assume that if mathematics is not understood then further time and practice is necessary. So it is with artistic learning, which (Chapter 2) can need repeated experience for ability to develop.

Very often we feel like giving up the effort just at the point where children are about to make a breakthrough in skill acquisition or artistic awareness. To be surrounded by children's artistic disasters, accept them and believe things really are about to get better, is a necessary ingredient for working with this age-range. Children do improve and learn to cope with very difficult problems in their artwork. But it cannot be emphasized too strongly that it does take time. In a group they can learn a great deal from each other provided a deliberate effort to find time to teach them is made.

Finding the best time to discuss an art project with children is sometimes difficult. There are, however, a number of ways of coping with this and they are all worth trying. If they ring familiar bells well and good. The alternatives suggested here are practical solutions which some teachers have found work for them.

(1) At the end of the morning, clear up for lunch, gather all the children round and explain what the afternoon art activity will be about. (With luck this gives some of them a chance to think about it over the lunch hour.) Not all children may do art, some will follow this up the next day.

(2) Set one group, the teaching group, new work (simple potato printing, for example). The other group practises tasks like colour-mixing, drawing, or pattern making. Then the groups change over halfway through the session. Next day they finish off work as one large group, or continue as two groups, or finish off work as individuals.

(3) Set one group the task of using the Book Corner, or reference library, to try a 'finding-out' game. For example, 'See how many round shapes you can find and write down the page numbers ... see how many different blues ... see how many different creatures you can find that have two legs.' (Builds up awareness of shape.)

(4) Let one group cut up pieces of coloured paper in preparation for working with collage materials. They need to create a reasonably useful pile of pieces. (Practice in using scissors − even measuring.) This should be a short activity as it can be uninteresting, but it does buy enough time to start off another group activity (which may not be art). It is then possible to return to the paper-cutting group to begin a collage and explain much more to them.

(5) Take one group which learned how to work with a different material yesterday and rearrange groups so that children work in pairs, one child showing the other how to use the new material.

(6) Explain an idea to three groups at the same time (for example, a drawing and painting project). Then change the rules for each group so that there are limitations on how each group uses materials. For example, one group might use only blacks, whites and greys. Another group might be told to choose one colour to emphasize rather than any

other, another group might not in the end use paints but take the same idea using coloured felt-tip pens. The purpose of this would be to use the results for further discussion on art and compare the different responses each group had.

(7) Introduce a new skill to the whole class rather than one group. Then when they come to do the group activity they already know something about it. They will need reminders, development and adjustment to the new skill, but this can be more profitable than explaining the same thing three times over, once for each group.

The Whole Class and the Group

Some teachers prefer to organize art for the whole class, which does not mean that they do exactly the same activity with every child, but that only art takes place within the classroom. This is not without its advantages because the focus can be very powerful as the children see what each other does and the teacher draws attention to what has happened. There are, as we might expect, serious limitations regarding space available and the kind of materials which can be used. Sometimes it is possible to arrange with a colleague to take a small group (a live-now-pay-later approach where we agree to take a very large group in return for having had a small one with which to work). There may be opportunities for a large group to work in the hall, or extend to the corridor, depending on the self-discipline of the children involved. Even so, children will inevitably need to share materials so that in effect the whole class will still find itself working in smaller groups. The focus of all the children is towards art and there may be greater opportunities for the development of social skills through sharing, tidying away, helping each other and learning to use space wisely.

The kind of larger group project which proves worthwhile is one where it is possible to make use of children's differing abilities. For example, in language children might make a class newspaper where the written or drawn contributions are of different size and complexity according to the contributors. The final product is a 'scissors and glue' assemblage and depends for its success on involving each child in an individual way. The outcome is then greater than the sum of its parts. In art, it is likely that only a few things lend themselves exactly to this approach. For there to be entirely individual contributions each child needs to work on a small part which finally pieces together to form the whole. If we contrast this with a frieze, someone has to design and cover the background on which are stuck the various contributions. Decisions are taken about where things are placed, and at that point it is very difficult for a teacher not to offer advice or interfere.

Despite this problem, a large-scale work (see Plate 12 and Plates 13 and 14) captures the attention and periodically provides a memorable experience for the participating children. Subjects commonly attempted are things like 'The Magic Garden', where each child contributes an imaginary exotic flower and where materials like tinsel, foil, bottle tops and objects can be stuck to a background. This is a useful experience for children to have, but how could such a project be developed further?

One interesting way is to use the exotic background which has been finished and gradually build out from it to make a garden on a table in front. Piece by piece the garden can grow to include junk models, Plasticine or claywork, paths, hedges and fences. Much depends on how a creative idea like this is used. For instance, there are a number of worthwhile discoveries to be made using either hedges or fences as a sub-theme. Children can design their own fences, look for differently shaped fences in the environment, or find out about the creatures and plant life which inhabit the hedgerows.

Organizing a mural where abstract pattern is used is slightly different. The children each have the opportunity to produce a unit, such as a tile-sized piece of work, which forms part of the final product. There are interesting choices to be made about colours and materials, and the source of the patterns can be very varied. In fact a pattern may grow from a previous mural idea so that development takes place from one large-scale piece to the next. The work may be three-dimensional but still using a unit as the basic form.

As with all group projects, the children may need to be made aware before the start of where their own unit fits in with the final product. Ideal projects are those in which each piece of contributory work is a variation on a theme. A simple example of this would be a theme of circles or stripes, where each child finds something which can be a stimulus for their part of the whole.

Since children frequently work on the same-sized paper as each other, it is likely that occasionally they produce work which can later be assembled into a mural, even if that was never the original intention. On the other hand, it might be necessary to organize the class into groups for discussion and pool ideas before planning a mural. The children might work on scraps of paper planning out their individual designs. Alternatively, an appropriate time to organize discussion groups could be at the assembling stage, where various arrangements for the final form could be tried out.

In contrast to a whole class project, which is put together as a group effort, pupils can work on murals in small groups. Sometimes large paintings or collages using sheets of brown wrapping paper are appropriate projects. However, there is no ideal fixed number of children to have working this way, though there are some combinations which do not seem to be successful. Four children working co-operatively works well, as does two. But six or more children all trying to do a frieze tends to produce group leaders and passengers. This can still provide good learning experiences though the social learning may outweigh the artistic development. Naturally, what determines decisions about group size is the nature of the project, the children there to do it, and the constraints in terms of space and organization of materials.

Organizing Materials

Although organizing materials involves personal preferences there are some ideas worth examining. Sinks, for example, are too often well away from the classroom and the design of many schools can stretch the ingenuity of teachers to the limit.

> The nearest sink is at the bottom of the corridor through a Fire Door which has a strong spring to keep it shut. I cannot possibly send a child to empty a bucket of water and for me to send children all that way to clean palettes is out of the question. We manage with two buckets and a lot of kitchen rolls ... painting ... yes it's messy but we do a lot of it and they learn to cope.
>
> (Deputy headteacher)

This particular teacher produced remarkable paintings from her children and her organization contributed substantially towards the success of her sessions. She was unable to do much colour-mixing on palettes but still managed some with small groups rather than none at all. When mixing colours was impossible, she provided up to eighteen different mixtures of colour in non-spill containers. At any one time there were about twelve colours being used and the children took these pots of colour from a trolley which had been wheeled into the centre of the room. There were various brushes of different sizes provided, one for each paint pot.

> They ask each other 'Have you got a thick blue?' by which they mean 'Is there a pot of blue with a thick brush in it?' They refer to thin yellows, thick yellows and so on according to the size of brush ... obviously there's a lot of sharing but it works. I sometimes have to keep returning pots to the trolley because the children forget but I don't mind that.

The same teacher often took all the chairs out of the room, even the tables, for a whole afternoon's painting. If the tables were still there, the children worked standing up and if the tables went, the floor was used. On her trolley was a shelf for a basket of brushes, some chalks, pencils, rubbers, glue with spreaders and a stack of palettes. Other materials were in boxes or racks and there was a bin which had wheels and contained bits and pieces for collage and junk modelling. A bench was full of materials, including felt-tipped pens, dyes with screwtop lids and oddments of paper.

A well-organized room which looks tidy and neat is by no means the best classroom. It may be so clean and tidy that it dissuades a teacher from using paint, thereby restricting what the children are allowed to do. But an untidy and disorganized classroom is certainly the worst. Materials are soon lost, damaged, or wasted, and the room reflects a poor standard of care. Children enjoy some form of social training in looking after their classroom and it is worthwhile teaching them to look after paints, brushes and similar equipment. The general emphasis on care affects other pieces of equipment throughout the school, such as musical instruments or maths materials. Where educational funding is unduly restricted, taking care is obviously important and affects the economy of the school.

The school day is punctuated by minor irritations which are connected with organization. Trivial details like counting scissors or pens can be made easier by making (or persuading someone else to make) racks for everything possible. Some teachers like children to practise their counting, but if that is not a priority, racks save a considerable amount of time and effort expended in needless counting.

Where water is being used it is dangerous practice to use glass jam jars. It is not worth the agony of searching for splinters of glass if they do break, let alone the risk of accidents to children's eyes. There are plenty of non-spill water pots on the market, some of them designed to be

Plate 1 My Mum. Age 4 yrs 6 mths. 620 x 425 mm
Princess. Age 5. 620 x 480 mm

Plate 2 Maze. Age 6. 300 x 210 mm

Plate 3 An Angry Face. Age 7. 500 x 400 mm

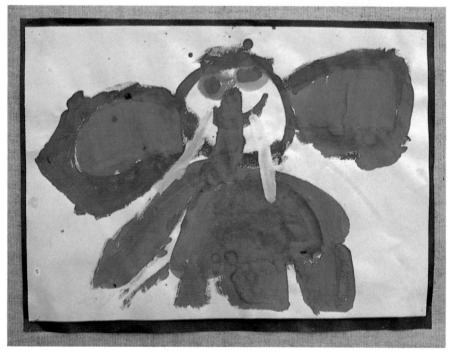

Plate 4 Elephant. Age 5. 580 x 420 mm

Plate 5 Lost Your Mum? – poster. Age 7/8. 280 x 400 mm

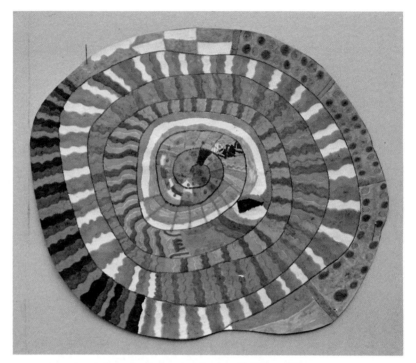

Plate 6   Patternwork. Age 7. 330 x 270 mm

A furious dilemma.

Plate 7   From *James and the Giant Peach* − story.
Age 6. 750 x 480 mm

Plate 8 From *James and the Giant Peach* — story.
Age 6. 750 x 480 mm

Plate 9 Tiger. Age 6. 280 x 205 mm

Plate 10   Violins. Ages 6, 7, 5.

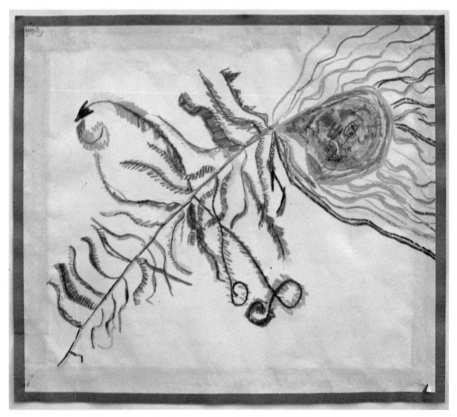

Plate 11   Feathers – drawing. Age 8. 280 x 330 mm

Plate 12　Fairground – group picture. Age 7/8. 2000 x 1500 mm

Plates 13, 14 A Thousand and One Nights. Ali Baba – group mural. Age 7/8.

Plate 15   Lowry Pictures. Age 7/8.

FROM THE PAINTING BY L.S.LOWRY

Plate 16   Looking at the Crust of a Loaf. Age 8. 180 x 137 mm

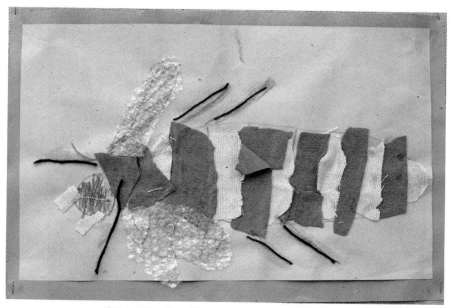

Plate 21　Bee Collage. Age 7. 500 x 300 mm

Plate 22　Castle – potato print. Age 7. 430 x 320 mm

extremely stable when knocked. Trays, trolleys, shelves, containers and racks are worth some experiment to find out what works best. The effort needed to do this is amply repaid in terms of energy saved over the term.

A popular idea is to create an 'Art Corner', or a 'Maths Bay', which can be useful as a way of tempting children to try out materials which are already there. It can be a space-saver which cuts down unnecessary movement around the classroom. A better description of it might be an 'Art Resource Area', an idea which conjures up the feeling that much more should be available than art materials. Twigs, plants, wall displays and organized materials make up an interesting corner to investigate.

This kind of organization is attractive and makes children feel secure, but it can also lead to inflexible arrangements of space. A handful of teachers become obsessed with the unchangeable arrangement of their room and would never dream of moving things around. Their art corners and mathematics bays hardly ever change. The 'Art Corner' is a good idea, so long as other arrangements are also tried out. Then it really is a resource, and not a regular dumping ground for children who have finished something else and are at a loose end.

Organizing Space and Time

A balancing act is often needed to judge between scale of work, space available and the time taken to complete artwork. These affect each other. It does not take long to work out that large sheets of paper, which occupy a great deal of space, obviously take longer to cover with paint or collage materials. Using large brushes and small paper, as compared with small brushes and large paper, has outcomes which are entirely opposite in terms of time. But more relevant is the way in which time is organized according to the specific activity being done. Whilst this kind of organization requires some experience and a few good guesses, there is no doubt that devising short activities which are like games is a useful way of balancing up the different work rates of individuals. Making art workcards about pattern, for example, or using up scraps of paper for drawing fantasy pictures (such as 'A Dancing Jelly', or 'A Melted Piano') is another way of making the sessions more flexible. The need to organize time should cause us to try out different approaches, none of which should become a fixed habit or ritual. Here are some further examples.

(8) Try to contrast detailed and lengthy discussion with giving a very

short introduction, followed by artwork, followed by stopping the class or group in order to discuss details at much greater length, followed by further work.

(9) Try three short practice activities like (a) a two-minute drawing, (b) trying out different pencils, (c) making ruler and pen patterns, followed by an extensive piece of work which uses all three practices.

(10) Stimulate two activities at the same time and allow the children to decide how much time to spend on each. For instance, children might draw a collection of fruit and also make Plasticine models of it at the same session. They would be thinking in two and three dimensions, leaving one, coming back to the other. (They must eventually finish both.)

(11) Give children a piece of paper which they are told has to last three days, be drawn on, added to, embellished and altered with a variety of materials including white paint or chalk. (This is one way of helping children to understand that artwork can change and develop.)

(12) Stop an art activity halfway through to play an observation game, then return to the activity. (This allows for children to take a mental break from their task and with luck come back to it with new energy.)

Space in the classroom and on work surfaces can be organized differently depending on the activity. The example of having a central trolley of materials has already been mentioned. But there are other ways of sharing out space so that materials are used to the best advantage. Children who are used to a formal arrangement of desks or tables take time to adjust to having their room reorganized. Yet they do benefit from trying different groupings of work surface. They might be working on a frieze where two long rows of desks put together is the answer. They might be doing a continuous pattern where each piece of paper joins on to its neighbour. A circle of joined tables might work best or a group of children using the full length of the corridor.

An experienced teacher develops a sense of organization which foresees most of the likely problems children will encounter. Despite this, children can still be seen trying to work on paper whilst placing paint pots, water pots or palettes on top of the work they are doing. They do not seem to have any natural inclination to use space well and often need to be shown how. It is staggering what they will endure even though it seriously restricts their ability to cope.

It is worth working out what the likely movements of children will be to see if the best arrangement of tables has been arrived at. Can some children work better standing up at easels? Would it be better to put some tables against the wall to leave more space for movement around the room? Is it worth having some folding tables which are used for art, possibly shared between classes?

> I'll have one group working in the corridor, with these large pieces of paper and chalk, drawing their pictures ... another group might be painting, and another group might be chalking on top of their finished pictures.
>
> (Deputy headteacher)

Organizing the rationing of time throughout the week is more awkward to envisage. The example which follows is not a curriculum model, simply a way of thinking about time in relation to subject areas.

> I organize what I call my 'thick sandwich' week. I like to think that each area of the curriculum is covered during the week ... that's the bread. The filling is what I particularly want to do that week ... one week we'll do a lot of science ... another week it's extra art, or maths, or language.
>
> (Deputy headteacher)

There are other ways of organizing time across a term, like running a two-week project, or a longer one still. They affect the available space for doing other things. Organizing a long-term project can have similar constraints on time and space as using the school hall, or the dining-room, might have. A project which takes up space and time usually displaces other activities. This and other variables need to be considered carefully even if some of them seem at first sight to be unimportant.

Organizing Wallspace

A feature of organizing a classroom is how wallspace is used, not only for display, but for siting various pieces of equipment. Although electric points can condition some of the organization, the classroom may be made far more workable and attractive if the siting of equipment is rethought. A natural tendency is to use equipment in the place it has always been available. But children's needs change and an occasional rethink is necessary. Apart from this, the appearance of the wall displays can be made to look very professional. In this respect there are one or two pointers to success. These also apply to exhibition space but are included here as simple guidelines to be tried out.

(1) Where possible, work should be mounted (e.g. on black paper) creating a margin around the work of not less than 10 mm. Use a trimmer or guillotine which cuts at right angles or the work may look square but prove not to be when the display has been assembled.

(2) Wallpaper used as a backing, especially if it has a strong colour or pattern, tends to detract from the display.

(3) Some attempt can be made when placing work on display to level the top edges of various pieces so they create a level top line to the whole display. Similarly the bottom edges of display boards can have work aligned.

(4) An alternative to this is to make up a symmetrical pattern with the pieces of work. The pattern should be spaced and balanced with a good margin around each piece of work. Avoid placing work at angles.

(5) A minimum space of 50 mm should be left around each piece of work to avoid overcrowding it. No work should hang over the edge of a display area.

(6) Titles or headings need only be few in number but should be well lettered. Using questions on displays often makes them far more useful, especially if they include visual aids and teaching resources, as well as children's work. Try any lettering aid you can find. Rule guidelines each time, even if you are experienced, and leave plenty of space round words. Paper can always be trimmed off later to leave a generous margin all round.

Sometimes good organization comes through the headteacher of the school. There are, despite traditional criticisms, excellent heads in each authority and many staff learn their organizational skills from them. Last-minute organization is inevitable during a busy working week. But there are many routine reorganizations of groups, space, time, wall-space, equipment and materials which are well worth experiment. Viewed individually these organizational details do not loom large. Collectively they permeate the whole ethos of the classroom and school, contributing to its smooth running, encouraging better discipline and ultimately enabling more efficient teaching to take place.

7

Talking With Children

Imaginative Talk

IN THE tale of Hansel and Gretel, two children find a house in the woods. The house is made of sweets, candies and chocolate. An imaginative delight for any child. The power of imagination lets us distort ideas, so that we can make things any colour we like in our mind's eye, or any size, or any combination of forms we fancy. For the children hearing the story of Hansel and Gretel, the house becomes edible as tempting materials are combined to function as a dwelling.

A surprisingly large amount of this imaginative thinking depends on our ability to accept and use quite unrelated ideas. An example might be for children to describe 'A Million Pound Ice-Cream', or 'Life on Top of a Cream Cake', both of which defy our usual concept of scale and value. They require an unusual sense of the infinitely improbable, yet imaginatively possible. It is as if anything we like can be drawn on the paper of the mind.

Imaginative talk can stretch children's thinking allowing them to create wild and weird pieces of artwork. Not only that, but it will probably help other areas of their learning, like their creative writing and problem-solving. By using their imagination they often generate a flow of creative ideas which can spill over into other parts of the curriculum. The impractical ones can always be rejected later on, leaving the best ideas for discussion and modification.

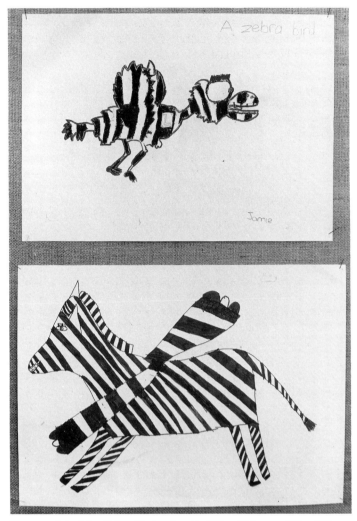

Figures 21, 22 Zebra Birds. Age 7. 430 x 300 mm, 450 x 320 mm

Stories are full of rich sources of imaginative imagery and children are used to listening to fantastic ideas locked into an impossible but believable logic. Imaginative questions, the more bizarre the better, can lead children to feel that imagination has some currency in the classroom. Discussion of mind-stretching visual ideas teaches children that their own fantasy is not only acceptable but can be used to great advantage in their artwork. In the realms of imagination, children play with combinations of images, making new relationships between them, enlarging, changing and adapting them to suit their fantasy. Examples of topics for imaginative talk, which can be tried to see how far children will stretch the unusual, could be to discuss:

(1) Do you know what a zebra looks like? Well, what do you think a Zebra Bird could be like?

(2) The highest mountain is Mount Everest. Imagine climbing a much higher model of someone's nose.

(3) The road in your street is probably a dull colour. Can you imagine it looking like a patchwork of coloured squares?

(4) What do you imagine a patchwork-coloured cat would look like?

(5) If you could live inside any object you like, what would you choose to live in? Why? What would it look like?

(6) What do you think would happen if all pavements were made of banana skins?

The famous painting, by René Magritte, of an enormous apple filling a corridor may be familiar. We can speculate on the question being asked, 'What do you think it would be like if an apple was so large it filled the whole corridor?' This, and many other imaginative paintings, make use of the impossible witty combination of ambiguous scale or size. The canvas of Magritte is partly the canvas of the mind, and there is a fragile line to be drawn between imagination, memory and the senses. Children will happily change from one to the other as they work (see Figure 6, Chapter 4).

The following idea was tried with some 7 year-olds and makes use of looking as well as imagining, switching from one state to the other.

THE IMAGINARY TREE

Concepts   Shape, pattern, line, adaptation.

Learning Potential   Use of observation, imagination, drawing ability, discrimination of structure.

Skills   Drawing, fine motor skills, selection of colours.

Stimulus   Begin by looking and talking with children about part of a tree. (Find a tree fragment, possibly a small piece of driftwood picked up from the beach. It might be weatherbeaten, knotted and twisted into an interesting shape.) The children are asked to describe what they can see. Then they have to think what they might add to their drawing of the fragment to make up an imaginary tree. The tree can have anything added they wish, can be coloured and patterned as they like, and may be any size. Discuss, elicit and develop ideas.

Options   Children could draw their tree on rough trial paper first or begin on a larger sheet. They might find their own (local) source of reference for part of a tree. Choice of viewpoint, choice of materials, size, content and components of tree (e.g. creatures, a 'tree den', nest, leaves, blossom). Site of tree (garden? wood? city?).

Materials   Choose from paint, crayon, coloured felt-tips, collage materials, pencils, black pen.

Practical Session   The children draw from the fragment itself, looking carefully for what they can see. When they have enough on paper to satisfy their need to have some basic shape, they add details (extra branches? leaves? blossom? spirals? tree bark?). They colour in what they have done, embellish a drawing, or begin to paint.

Development   The subject could change to 'Who inhabits the tree?' and children also bring in objects to which they themselves could add ideas. These could be natural forms or man-made. Alternatively, the theme could develop into topics related to their bringing in, for example, a broken mechanical alarm clock or part of a machine. These become 'An Imaginary Machine', 'A Robot', 'The Workings of My Head', or 'A New Vehicle'.

There are other areas of imagination like dreams and nightmares to touch on. Some children may find these too disturbing to talk about but many will welcome the chance to bring the images of dreams into their artwork. Even if dreams and nightmares never become part of artistic expression, they form a valuable source of shared experience, not least because they involve children's feelings. There are many children for whom the images of dreams in art are a way of expressing their most feared anxieties. Often art becomes a vehicle for talking about such influential experiences as those involving parents, themselves, violence, love or loss.

Of course, not all discussion need centre on the extreme, zany or dreamlike state of imagination. Memory, that unreliable window of the mind, proves to be a constant resource for discussion of imagery. The artists Henry Moore and Ben Nicholson used to play a memory game called 'Shuteye Golf', where they drew a map of a golf course on a sheet of paper. They practised their memory of the golf course by trying to find their way round it using a pencil, but without looking. They had to negotiate hazards like cows and bunkers, gaining or losing points accordingly. The claim was that the game improved spatial memory. Memory games played with children can take many forms, of which the best known is probably the one played at parties where several objects are put on a tray and the children have to say, when the tray is hidden from view, what was there. Such memory games tend to be classed as an entertainment, but they can be played more seriously as a way of teaching children to develop their visual memories.

Discussion of memories can be made specific. Memory of shape can be encouraged by asking children to describe from memory what particular shape they think things are, then, where possible, comparing the description with the original source of reference. The process is a straightforward one. With practice children can learn to compare with shapes, sizes, lengths and characteristics that they know they can talk about. Playing memory games is rarely ever wasted time and can be fitted in during those odd five-minute periods when children are waiting to do something else. Apart from this, there may be the chance, for example, to visit a wood, or go on a school trip, which can provide the opportunity to discuss and memorize leaf shapes or visual details of the journey. Such discussion is a necessary contrast to the more usual gathering of information which goes on.

Using Questions

One of the more obvious ways an interested teacher interests her children is through the comments made throughout the school day. These range from questions to discussion, including commands, instructions and a great deal of factual information. Art, as has been pointed out, does not readily lend itself to facts and has (Chapter 2) been described as a 'wordless' experience. But talking with children about their perceptions is unavoidable if we seriously want to develop their abilities. A distinction must also be made between talking *with* children and talking *to* them. Whether we act as benign dictator, democrat, or combinations of both, discussion with children provides us with valuable and necessary feedback. We do, after all, need to understand children's responses in order to make informed decisions about our own teaching.

Frequently, teachers ask children questions which arise from the work which is already going on. In mathematics, for instance, there is a mathematical language and mathematical concepts. Just as elaborate questioning can be appropriate for mathematics teaching, so with art there are a number of important areas of teacher and pupil exchange. Quite apart from talking about paint, paper and images, there are (Chapter 2) the well-established formal elements, such as colour, line, shape, pattern, tone and texture. We tend to think of these mostly relating to artwork, yet they exist in almost everything we see around us and can be applied to looking at the environment just as well as drawing or painting.

For the purpose of making this clear, we can analyse some questions and search for those which are clearly visual in their characteristics. What follows here may be familiar, yet it bears closer examination because in many classrooms, the use of 'visual questions' is often mis-understood or entirely absent.

Imagine we are examining a slice through a tomato. The question 'How

Figures 23, 24   Violin Drawings. Age 6. 220 x 323 mm, 295 x 395 mm

many seeds can you see?' is not necessarily a visual category of question. 'What shape and colour do you think they are?' comes closer. 'What colours do you think you could mix to make the colour of those seeds?' pushes the question towards the use of art materials. These last two questions point to a fundamental function of art teaching. A teacher can consciously and deliberately bring visual and art-oriented details of the environment to children's notice.

Ideally everything should come from the children. But they do need prodding in a direction which allows this to happen. When this is successful, teachers extend children's vision whilst taking full account of what they offer. For example, in a class of 6 year-olds, the children are gathered round their teacher looking at a violin together (see Figures 23 and 24 and Plate 10).

Teacher: Let's have a close look at it ... a careful look at it. Tell me some of the things you can see.
Paula: An 'S' and an 'F'.
Teacher: These are called 'F' holes and the sound comes out here (points) ... what else can you see?
Aaron: Knobs at the top ... string things.
Teacher: (pointing) These are pegs and round them go the strings ... what are the strings like?
Jodi: They're straight.
Michael: (interrupts) I know what's curved at the top.
Teacher: (ignoring him) Are all the strings the same?
Kelly: No, some of them are thick and some thin. (Teacher talks about sound and plucks strings.)
Teacher: Now if we look at the shape does it remind you of anything?
Toni: Yeh, a guitar.
Michelle: Like a pear shape.
Teacher: See, the curve comes out here ... then goes in ... can you see? ... Michael ... you're looking at the back ... what can you see?
Michael: It's got stripes on it.
Michelle: And that bit there (points to top pegs) goes round and round.
Teacher: We can call that a spiral shape. Let's draw a spiral in the air. Start in the middle and go round ... (Children do this.)
Paula: It's like a snail shell.

(Later on the children are drawing.)

Michelle: Violins aren't all sorts of colours.

Lisa: Well mine is.

Aaron: They're all sorts of different browns.

Teacher: What do you think you've missed out from your drawing?

Toni: The neck and the curvy bit ... I need a brown ... I need a brown ... you got a brown?

Michelle: Where's the orange? ... I need a brown ... I'm using this one because that's shiny there.

Here we have a good example of how children make comparisons and analyse shapes and colours. Their teacher steers them from general observations to specific comparisons of detail and generates interest by talking about the shapes that they can see. She also extends their experience by making them think about several qualities they would need to consider if they began drawing the instrument. The emphasis on visual detail is necessary to encourage concentrated looking and build up a strong mental image, which then acts as a basis for drawing and colouring. Of course, this is not a matter of telling children what details to include in their drawings. Rather than this, it is to engage children's attention in so many details that they are compelled to exercise choice about what they want to draw.

When this teacher asked 'What do you think you've missed out from your drawing?' there was no intention of providing answers. The decision was theirs, by which route far more original work can be forthcoming. Later on that day, more was said about the sound of the violin and the teacher played a recording of some violin music. The children practised letter shapes and wrote words and sentences connected with their experience of the instrument. Their comments and questions were wide-ranging in comparison with the visual ones introduced before the children began drawing. An interesting feature, however, was that they drew first, then wrote, rather than the other way round.

The process of looking and questioning has an added bonus for the teacher. Together, teacher and child can talk in terms which build a vocabulary for looking at things. Both of them sharpen observation by sharing what they themselves see. Before long, and really with little prompting, children become very good at describing the appearance of what they see. The teacher might have stimulated interest in the first place, but she soon discovers that children are very ready to respond. They can analyse what they are looking at even to the extent of including comments on specific qualities they find, like shapes being spiky, smooth, winding, curved, or twisting.

Sometimes the children learn to find a 'visual vocabulary' of shapes in what they see, not in words as such, but as letter shapes.

> We talk about line, what a line can do and where it's going ... up, down, sideways, or perhaps in spirals ... I teach my children a vocabulary of letter shapes ... letter families when they can manage capital letters ... 'E', 'H', 'L', 'T', 'V' or 'S' shapes ... they can be found in patterns and shapes ... They're all around and finding them gives my children a confidence in drawing.
>
> (First school teacher)

Usually the children can find a letter 'L' or a 'V' in something. And though this way of looking should not become a rigid method it does help them to focus attention on shape. The angles of doors, desks, windows, boxes and chairs are examples of source material for finding letters. A further development is also to ask

Is that letter 'V' the same as this one? How is it different?

By this means the children gradually build up a strongly differentiated framework which helps them to look even more carefully than they previously did. Once they try to find different 'L's, (and more importantly, recognize the differences) they are making very sophisticated comparisons indeed. A start has been made which is no different in kind from that made by many artists down the centuries. It is said that the painter Cézanne often looked for circles, squares and cubes in his own paintings. Comparison with known shapes is nothing new, but it may be very new to those children who have never had the chance to try it out.

Through discussion, children often give back what we give out to them. If, for example, we spend a whole week periodically looking out at the different shapes and colours to be seen in the sky, before very long the children begin talking about the changes that they have seen. The following days and weeks are often times when they recount memories of clouds seen the previous evening or perhaps during a weekend rainstorm. This vision regularly finds new expression in their paintings, where the colours they see and the shapes they create become as absorbing as the skies they are trying to paint.

Naturally, apart from all the discussion that is possible, there are times when to talk with children is actually detrimental to their progress. Once they have been stimulated to work with art materials, children need to be left alone to get on, especially at the earliest stages of development. They may well feel apprehensive, but so do many artists when they make their first marks on canvas. If children do not think they are expected to make a start by themselves, they often engineer ploys for extra help. The extra help is almost entirely unnecessary at this stage and to offer them further help simply puts off the moment when they have to start. If they regularly needed more and yet more help, they would never do anything by themselves. As a general habit it is good practice to walk away and leave them to start by themselves. They quickly take in the message that they are on their own.

Later on, when the work is well under way, if we were never to comment and feed in encouragement, we would find ourselves teaching in a rather ineffective way. Some teachers would say that to talk to children about their artwork in progress is to over-influence it, whilst others find questions can be well handled and constructive. Teachers are rightly more cautious about commenting for fear of harshly criticizing, destroying a child's fragile confidence, or stereotyping the work. But fear of being insensitive can lead to giving praise as the only apparent safe response. Yet it is a response which bewilders a pupil who is not having much success. How often does a teacher lose credibility this way as well as the opportunity to teach something useful? Without support and encouragement we know that children lose heart, but need the encouragement be so vague? Are there other areas of comment which are important?

Commenting on Children's Work

The age of the computer-controlled robot is with us and if pursued thoughtlessly, the ideas which follow might be more like a computer's response than that of a human being. Certainly if we followed each idea in sequence the effect would be mechanical. Yet the categories suggested here need not be used inflexibly. They only describe the most likely areas we have for contact with any group of children about the artwork they are doing, yet provide a marked contrast to the unending vague praise children's work generally elicits. We can talk about

(1)   what we asked the children to do
(2)   further ideas around the theme on which they are working
(3)   feelings evoked by the artwork
(4)   their use of fantasy and imagination
(5)   shapes, colours, patterns, lines, tone, texture
(6)   scale, size, arrangement of the design

(7)   use of materials

(8)   a particular technique

(9)   the effort put in

(10)   ways ideas could be used in another medium another time.

Praising the use of well-mixed colour, careful attention to shape, or control of materials are obvious enough areas to warrant praise for most children. Few teachers have not experienced circumstances where they want to praise a pupil who is having difficulty, simply to spur him on. An experienced teacher finds ways of commenting that are not immediately judgemental. For example, the comment 'That's better than yesterday's work' is a safe area for praise, whilst 'That's good' can sometimes sound rather generalized and unconvincing by comparison. Fortunately, few pupils quite know, or remember well enough, how good yesterday's work was.

There is little doubt that rewards such as approval or praise are valuable motivators. But children usually want to please and will respond to our own personal values and judgements. There is no way entirely to avoid influencing children, and if we had no influence on children would we honestly believe we were teaching? Comments can have a positive motivating effect if they are well aimed and specific. An effective example of ways to encourage would not just be to say something global such as, 'I like that', but to add a particular dimension such as, 'I like the way you have

drawn that shape ...

added those details ...

arranged this on the paper ...

mixed those colours ...

chosen those colours ...

tried to remember what that looked like ...

found that pattern ...

worked on your own ...

worked together ...

glued this, cut that ...

threaded these together.'

Searching for rewarding things to say to children has a secondary spin-off of teaching us to look for special qualities in their work. It also helps children to understand some of the values and qualities which are to be found in what they do. Sadly, a great deal of comment from teachers tends of necessity to be on a very mundane level of organization and control of materials. This is true of many activities (see Bennett *et al.*, 1984). The valuable creative component which is specific rather than general can include rewards which have some credibility in our eyes and those of the children.

Questions can swiftly follow on from rewards. Superficially they may have the flavour of an evaluation but effectively they encourage children to think about what they are doing. Questions can be challenges which spur children on to find out more, such as

'How did you mix that colour?'
'What do you think about … ?'
'Where did you see this?'
'Can you see how … ?'
'Can you think of another way of … ?'
'What else could you add to … ?'
'What would you do next time if … ?'
'How do you feel about … ?'

In any busy class, possibly with over thirty children, time for talking with them is precious. Which is all the more reason for making discussion purposeful. There may be no immediate goals. A question like 'What other way can you think of doing this?' may not actually produce any answer but can be asked with the purpose of making children think about what alternatives there might be. That in itself makes the use of unanswerable questions educationally worthwhile, even if personally we would rather there were always answers.

An Artistic Vocabulary

Children learn to use words like shape, colour and line, if their teacher refers to them with some frequency. But there are a variety of specialist words which children may also enjoy using. From some teachers they may pick up words like exquisite form, embellish, or clever design. Children love to use these special words even if they do not really understand them at first, so that words like medium, media, vermilion, umber, ultramarine, mobile, sculpture, spectrum, collage, mural, or ceramics can become part of their growing artistic vocabulary. Whether this vocabulary should develop by chance or by choice is a matter for individual teachers. But the most likely route for learning by choice is through looking at work done by other artists, even if this is artwork done by children.

Here, especially by seeing the work of famous artists, they can begin to develop critical awareness of what artists do (see Plate 15). It is almost impossible to talk with children about a reproduction of a work of art without them learning some special words to describe it. The words they use may be their own inventions, like 'curvy', or 'scratchy', but might also include technical words the teacher has taught them. Words like glaze, brushwork, scale, impact, balance, or expressive, are examples.

Four very useful areas in which to discuss a work of art are these (identified by Gaitskell and Hurwitz, 1970):

(1) What do you see? (Description)

(2) How are things put together? (Analysis)

(3) What is the artist trying to say? (Interpretation)

(4) What do you think of it? (Judgement)

Question three may provoke the most interesting responses and can be a problem for some teachers. How irresistible it could be to tell children what the artist was trying to say, rather than asking them first. The point of looking at artwork is to become practised at looking at it and develop some critical skills. The sophistication of expressive content in a work of art may take years to understand. Yet the categories suggested here are useful as a starting point for looking at work, though initially we should not expect them to produce much in the way of a response.

There is not much point knowing what the colours of the rainbow are unless they also have some meaning. Similarly, there is little to be gained from children's learning new words for everything in sight, just for the sake of doing so. Complementary colours, colour wheels, or the nuances of perspective can be spoken about, it is true. But impressive though knowledge of them might seem, they could obscure the real reasons for talking with children about their art. The main purpose of discussion is to involve children in building up their skills in verbalizing, visualizing and remembering. Even if the words used are very unsophisticated ones, the aim is to vitalize children's imagery and expression so that they are sufficiently confident in talking about their ideas, as well as working them out in a practical art medium.

8

Activities for Young Children

WE LIVE in a throw-away society where two years in the life of a home computer labels it old, or even obsolete. Children's individual need for a wide range of activities is insatiable and in the classroom they sometimes expect that what they did in art sessions yesterday should not be repeated. To repeat the experience would be instant boredom. Consequently, trying to persuade them that by doing things more than once they will develop artistically, can be an uphill struggle. That is, of course, if we have unwittingly taught them to expect novelty to be the keynote of their artistic learning.

This expectation can be passed on to children in two ways. The first is by regularly attempting to provide an endless variety of materials, so that nothing seems to be used twice; the second, by stimulating children with an entirely different idea each time they do art. Materials are rarely in plentiful supply, and if we try to deliver according to expected limitless variety, we will soon disappoint a lot of children. In any case, the special materials we buy need to be rationed if stocks are to last to the end of the year. There is some value in ringing the changes and presenting a new medium to children. But problems arise if the starting point (see Chapter 5) is always different materials rather than extension of ideas. As for stimulating an entirely new idea each time, it might be thought that doing so should be compulsory. There is nothing more boring than repeating ideas. Yet (Chapter 5) a distinction must be made between those ideas which are linked, such as themes, and the isolated, one-off art activities.

A regular diet of totally unrelated ideas and assorted materials makes for a very superficial art experience. Some semblance of continuity of thought and learning is not only desirable but sensible, given the complexities of an average school day. Extending ideas through themes, and making links with the rest of the curriculum, has too great a learning potential to be missed. In practice, young children most frequently draw, crayon and paint in response to the things they see (Plate 16), or their imagination and memory (Plates 7, 8). Yet both of these areas are not difficult to weave into ongoing themes, and it can be expected that children will benefit from linking one idea and another. Of course, there are occasions when using a new material is very stimulating. Even so, the specially different materials are best brought out of the cupboard when they are suited to an appropriate idea.

Ingredients

We can think of devising art activities as being like making a creative cake. We can change the ingredients and even the recipe to make a better cake, and if everything is skilfully blended, the result will be tasty and look delicious. The art activities suggested here will all work in the classroom. But structure, sequencing, discussion and the principles so far mentioned must be considered and implemented. Otherwise, the worst imaginable, tasteless and superficial artwork may be produced despite the very best of ingredients. There really is no such thing as a foolproof recipe for success.

At the reception age, 'play' activities are an obvious starting point. Yet 'play' is not in fact a very good word for what happens. Children may think they are playing but that is to underestimate the development that takes place. We may feel 5 year-olds are playing with art materials, but the resulting drawings and paintings are an important reflection of their interests and egocentric selves. Periodically there are signs of development in images, in ability to use materials and in awareness of space on the paper. Beyond this 'play' stage of activity, as children become less egocentric, the subject matter of their artwork is more diverse. To produce the very best artwork we still need to let them begin with play, and more important still, observe and listen to their response to their own world.

It may come as no surprise that playing with colours, playing with lines, playing with shapes and playing with paints are also the games of most adult artists. In any creative learning activity, we never quite stop playing, especially when materials are new. Most things are new to children and they need to learn through play long before they can develop any skills. In the 'Me' world (Chapter 4) of the 5 year-old, activities such as playing with art materials can typically absorb children in subjects like 'Me at School', 'Me in the Car', 'My Lunchtime', 'My Bedtime', 'My House', 'My Mum', 'My Dad', or 'My Dog'.

Whether or not activities are suited to a particular age-group depends on children's interests and their ability to cope. An understandable example is that of finger painting, which is often a 3 year-old's first opportunity to paint. Here the determining factors as to suitability are his undeveloped skill in controlling paint, and a toddler's need to explore new materials in a tactile way. Very young children enjoy finding out through touch as much as sight. They will often place things against their cheek to feel them, or examine them by mouth and by exploration in their hands.

As adults we are inclined to take the sense of touch for granted. Yet we know that anyone who is blind can describe the most complicated of forms through their own tactile experience of them. For young children, activities which include the experience of working with dough, clay, Plasticine and tactile objects are vital to their development. They delight in discovering that clay is malleable and can be enjoyed for its own sake. They twist, roll, thump and push dough about to feel what happens. They enjoy playing games where objects are hidden in a 'Feely-box', where they have to discover what the object is by touch.

Tactile experiences, play and exploration of materials new to children feature very strongly as characteristics of the 3 to 5 year-olds' art activity. Their attention span is very short and it is entirely justifiable to organize artwork so that there is a good measure of freedom in their artistic play. But that does not mean they do as they please. Each activity should be designed with learning in mind, even if practice in using materials is the sole objective. Inevitably, apart from artistic learning, language development can evolve as different subject matter begins to appear in the artwork.

Beyond exploratory play, the search for interesting subject content can always begin with the children themselves. One well-known way is to bring something into the classroom and generate a response as they touch it, look at it, discuss it and draw it. Traditionally, this might be anything from a wild plant, animal, natural form, museum specimen, clay model, to a piece of household equipment. The important activity is that of looking and responding. Another well-tried approach is to exercise children's imagination through stories (Plates 13, 14), but there are intriguing activities which are alternatives to these well-known ones.

Finding-out Activities

These examples are designed to encourage looking and imagining. There is no final artwork involved and they may be used as games or could be developed into longer-term projects. Much depends on how well they are presented to children. Some of them should be of very short duration if they are to be interesting, otherwise they need to be developed into specific art projects or changed to fit other areas of the curriculum.

EXAMPLE 1. FINDING OUT FROM PHOTOGRAPHS

Learning Potential Develops discrimination of shape. Exercises children's observation skills. Has potential of extending to observation (and development of visual memory) of the outside world.

Materials Old colour supplements, newspapers, ball-point pen, strong dark pencil or felt-tipped pen, scissors (optional).

Activity Children choose photographs from the magazines or newspapers. They cut them out (as carefully as they can), search for circles, triangles, squares and rectangles. With felt-tip or ball-point, they outline these on the photographs.

Development for Art Sessions Children exchange their findings with other children for checking or discussion/comparison. Found shapes are filled in to make them more obvious. Children draw a diagram copied from their outlines drawn on the photographs. Search for shapes is extended to the room, school, people. Quick drawings made, temporary displays, discussion by the teacher with her class.

EXAMPLE 2. LOOKING FOR LINES

Learning Potential Fosters awareness of line directions, thicknesses, complexity, angles and edges.

Materials Plain notepaper and pencil, pen.

Activity Depending on age and ability, children count the number of objects in the classroom which they can see have lines. Stripes, straight lines (edges of tables, books, window frames, doors, switches). Curved lines (chair backs?), printed or drawn lines, string, wire. Or they write down the names of objects which they think have lines. Or they look in their wordbooks (personal vocabulary books) to see how many things might have lines, stripes, or edges. They make a list from these words (no extra words needed).

Development for Art Sessions Extend to other parts of the school. Make drawings using lines they can find. Try out different line-making tools, pens, pencils, crayons. Look for lines as decoration and pattern. Create patterns with lines. Look specifically for stripes. Extend to 'Stripes' as a theme rather than a short activity (Chapter 5).

EXAMPLE 3. COLOUR-MATCHING ACTIVITY

Learning Potential Discrimination of colour. Awareness of shades and specific colour qualities.

Materials Scraps of coloured paper or cloth. These should be differing shades, like the kind best found in decorators' shade cards, materials catalogues, or objects brought in by the teacher. Pencil, paper.

Activity Children try to match the sample piece of colour they are given. They compare parts of book illustrations, scraps from magazines, each other's clothing, maths equipment, objects in the room. They note down (depending on ability) page numbers, the number of matches they find, names of objects, or make collections if practicable. Discussion of colour qualities, comparison in accuracy of matching.

Development for Art Sessions Extend to sorting shades into groups (e.g. three collections of different blues). Collected paper used for collage, mosaics. Children make a display of each collection. School/ class embarks on a 'Colour' project.

EXAMPLE 4. SURFACES

Learning Potential   Awareness of pattern qualities, surface colour, surface textures.

Materials   Paper, large black or brown wax crayon, notepaper, pencil.

Activity   Children list names of objects in the classroom which have same surface, e.g. using words like shiny, smooth, undulating. (Or describe if they are unable to make a list.) Make rubbings.

Development for Art Sessions   Children make small scrap-paper drawings of markings on surfaces, look in books for animals/birds, which have special markings on their coat, skin, or feathers. Create their own surface patterns based on the rubbings they make. Flood the rubbings with dye or light-toned ink (wax-resist technique). Make displays, use rubbings as collage material.

EXAMPLE 5. WHAT HAPPENS TO SHADOWS?

Learning Potential   Understanding of light and shadow. Awareness of change in appearances. Science of light.

Materials   Pencil, paper. Light source alternative to the sun (e.g. slide projector).

Activity   If the sun shines, children observe, discuss, draw effect of changes to objects which remain in the same position (e.g. things on the window ledge). Alternatively, teacher moves light source around objects so children observe shadow changes. Observation, discussion of effect of shadow which crosses wall and floor.

Development for Art Sessions   Children make a chart showing changes to shadow lengths, directions. Shadows idea becomes a project for class. Drawings, paintings, collages of shadow effects (sometimes without the objects needing to be drawn, i.e. shadows only). Work with black paper cut-outs representing shadows. Overhead projector? Shadow puppets? New theme, 'What Happens to Reflections?'

Variations of most of these 'Finding-out Activities' are not difficult to imagine. Matching shades of colour, possibly a five-minute game, can alternatively be translated into matching of shapes. For example, children can match clothing colours and patterns as they are waiting to go out of the classroom. Such useful exercises in discrimination of colour pay dividends as they permeate the children's artwork, and when art projects are under way, these games, exercises and activities can usefully be recalled. They provide teachers with the opportunity to remind children of the matching, sorting and comparing activities they have done. By this means the children's visual memory is jogged into action, making these short activities a valuable working resource.

Sometimes, with hindsight, an experienced teacher knows that valuable teaching ideas have been thrown away. A common enough experience, especially when first becoming a teacher, is to have planned ideas well but not exploited them to the full. There is no substitute for experience, and a skill worth developing is that of presenting ideas for art activities so that they have the maximum impact. Not giving children too many different new things to think about at once is an obvious help, but would it be better sometimes to hold back part of the more complex explanation and introduce it later? To sequence the stimulus to the activity is important if detailed explanation is necessary. Otherwise the children hear only a fraction of what we would like them to and often rush ahead without thinking. A question to consider is whether or not the children need to try things out on scraps of paper first, as a warm-up to the main activity. Alternatively, we may need to devise practice activities which are a prelude to a more ambitious project.

The following activities will need presenting with care so that children become very involved in and interested by them. No activity is absolutely perfect for every known group of children. Each activity needs adapting to fit the circumstances of the session. The structure used here includes a few alternatives from which to choose, which is no more than we would ask of the children we expected to do them.

Extended Activities

EXAMPLE 6. MAZES (FIGURE 2, PLATE 2)

Concepts   Line, pattern, shape, function.

Learning Potential   Problem-solving, design, use of imagination, discrimination of shape, language development.

Skills   Drawing, fine motor skills.

Stimulus   Begins in drama. Teacher discusses with children to see what knowledge they already have. Children act out themes on the 'Maze' topic, mythical beasts, being trapped or lost, finding gold, treasure.

   Discussion before using art materials. What is it like to see a maze from inside it, from a helicopter looking down, from the maze entrance? Meeting nasties along the route, finding treasure? Discussion about walled mazes, hedges, a playground maze – detailed descriptions from children about brickwork, hedges, colour. Ghost mazes, computer mazes, puzzles in books. Amazing mazes.

Options   Trial drawings of mazes that function in plan – scraps of paper. Choice of viewpoint, choice of materials. Decisions about size/ scale, content (how big?). Could it be in a garden? a city? a large estate? a funfair? Narrow, wide pathways? Movement, e.g. spiral?

Materials   Choose from coloured felt-tips, paint, crayons, card, scissors, scraps of paper.

Practical Session   Working from the stimulus, children make decisions about materials they should use, consider options available and use their imagination to produce a whole variety of personal mazes. Experience shows that ideas associated with this project can emerge spontaneously in other areas of the curriculum.

Development   Children gather round to make a combined maze using a large sheet of paper placed on the floor. Children add strips of black paper to make a route for the maze. Each child has only two strips of paper. Some children have task of making false trails. Finished maze is glued and displayed. Work then moves to writing, further drama. Solve a riddle to find your way? Children make their own black and white paper collage mazes. Maps? Displayed. Drama: with partners (one blindfolded), one giving descriptions and directions for a path through a maze, in hall, open space.

EXAMPLE 7. 'MULTI-COLOURED' COLOUR-MIXING (PLATE 17)

Note: depends on previous colour-mixing experiences.

Concepts Awareness of colour and shades of colour.

Learning Potential Discrimination of colour, use of imagination/ memory, control of medium. Comparisons of tone (dark and light).

Skills Mixing, drawing, painting. Control of clean water/paint.

Stimulus Begins in fantasy. Imagine a plateful of multi-coloured spaghetti? Imagine multi-coloured knitting? Imagine a sweet jar of multi-coloured jelly beans? Imagine a magic multi-coloured carpet?

Discussion with children to try to get them to think of multi-coloured fantasies. What might it look like? Can you remember objects which are different reds? Can you think of objects which are different greens? Greys? Muddy browns? How big on your paper? Try to elicit ideas from children, explore and develop their artistic vocabulary.

Options Try mixing on newspaper or scraps first. Limit colours, then gradually introduce more. Try different-sized brushes. Try short strokes/long strokes. Encourage mixing different dabs of colour. Encourage blending colours (using brushes, fingers, rubbing). Dots of colour.

Materials Paints, newspaper, coloured papers, crayons, pencils, brushes, mixing trays or plates/biscuit tin lids, water pots.

Practical Session The children experiment and explore colour-mixing, depending on previous experience the teacher may need to help with basic skills/mixing colour thickly enough.

Development Children sort through paint manufacturers' colour charts. Use for mosaics. Evolve 'Colour' displays, tables, rainbows, writing, music (e.g. 'The Multi-Coloured Music Bus'). Reawaken fantasy (e.g. 'Spotty Multi-Coloured Monsters').

EXAMPLE 8. COLOUR ON BLACK

Note: a development from Example 7.

Concepts   Colour awareness in relation to black. Awareness of tone (light/dark) in relation to black.

Learning Potential   Discrimination of tones and colours. Learning to handle white as an important colour. Comparison of colour on different toned surfaces.

Skills   Mixing (much more difficult to control mixtures of white on black). Keeping water pots clean enough to mix light colours. Mixing paints thickly enough for colour to be seen against black paper. Organizing mixing trays/dishes. Drawing.

Stimulus   Children imagine dark settings, skies at night? Outer space? Darkened caverns, rooms? Colour which is light enough to be seen is discussed, e.g. fireworks, lights, spaceships, planets, jewels? Discuss with children how it feels to be in a dark place – evoke memories, dreams.

Options   Try small pieces of black practice-sized paper. Use dark brown, dark grey, dark green, dark blue, instead of black. Deliberately try out colour which is too thin/too dark/badly mixed. Encourage children to develop own brushstroke styles.

Materials   Paints, palettes, brushes, water pots, black paper and chalk.

Practical Session   Children could work individually, or in pairs, or in small groups. This would involve discussion, joint decision-making and problem-solving.

Development   Extend to drama, building environments, imaginary dark places. Introduce 'simple science' of light, colour? Write stories?

Sing, play? Read? Imagine? Try out same colours against different backgrounds? Topics — e.g. 'People Who Lived in Caves'. Underground caverns, stalagmites? 'The Bottom of the Ocean'.

EXAMPLE 9. PACKAGES (PLATE 19)

Concepts Design development and organization of space/surfaces. Awareness of two- and three-dimensional shapes.

Learning Potential Translation of three-dimensional package into two-dimensional form. Understanding of design concepts in commercial products. Decision-making over drawing media, organization of space.

Skills Drawing of letter shapes in specific styles. Control of colouring media. Organization and placing on paper.

Stimulus Begins by looking at household products — breakfast cereal packets, soap boxes, shampoo boxes or plastic containers. Consider shapes, colours, backgrounds, lettering, size, organization of designs on folded and unfolded card packages.

Options Children can collect these packages, teacher may provide. Children may choose to draw in pencil, crayon, felt-tips, pen. Paper size may vary according to packages or cartons used.

Materials Cartons, packages, glue, glue spreaders, scissors, felt-tips, crayons, coloured and lead pencils, pens, assorted papers.

Practical Session Children make drawings of chosen package, container, or carton, carefully noting style, lettering, etc. This is then mounted together with the original package on a backing paper or displayed on the wall. Children are able to choose drawing materials.

Development Children design their own carton or package to advertise an imaginary product, e.g. Whizzo Washing Powder, Non-Spill Unbreakable Milk Bottles, Instant Beefburger Maker, Everlasting Ice-Creams. Children design posters using lettering from packages to advertise, e.g. Jumbo Jelly Factory, Amazing Beans Ltd. Advertise school meals? Class assemblies? Discuss television adverts?

EXAMPLE 10. BLACK AND WHITE PROJECT

Concepts   Pattern, shape, awareness of tone (dark and light).

Learning Potential   Problem-solving, increasing visual perception, shape discrimination, comparison of tone.

Skills   Sticking, paint-mixing. Control of clean water (important when using black paint). Control of paint.

Stimulus   Pictures, stories of 'Black and White', stripes, spots, patterns, e.g. *Black Bear, White Bear* by T. Harriott and L. Kopper. Books with illustrations entirely in black and white, direction of stripes? Create a mind-picture of a black and white fantasy creature? More black than white? More white than black? Dalmatians? Zebras? Zebra crossings? White snowflakes on tarmac. Newspapers. Coal/snow. Lights, holes.

Options   Choice of materials, choice of shapes: making patterns with shapes. Limit choice to two shapes? Three? Ready-cut shapes? Children cut?

Materials   Choose from black and white papers, card, scissors, glue, mixing trays, water, brushes, water pots, paints.

Practical Session   Working from the stimulus, children discuss with their teacher what materials are appropriate and consider the options available. Using imagination, children create patterns (using paints or sticking paper). Children draw with a brush or arrange shapes freely on paper. Goal is to try to create a pattern which leaves half the paper showing.

Development   Patterns where three-quarters of paper is covered. Construction of fantasy creatures, recalling stories. 'Black and White in Everyday Life': e.g. sweets, humbugs, liquorice allsorts — sorting according to pattern. 'Night and Day.' Collages using different kinds of blacks, whites (these vary slightly according to what kind of paper and paint is chosen). Children make collections of different black and white objects.

EXAMPLE 11. MAGIC-SPELL PATTERNS

Concepts   Pattern, line, colour.

Learning Potential   Imagination development, pattern invention, control of pattern, line, colour.

Skills   Drawing, colouring.

Stimulus   Magic Spell reading. Teacher reads, children read:

>Frog of eye and Bat of wings,
>Change round all the usual things,
>Pocus-Hocus patterns grow,
>Cover all the things I know.

Options   Choice of drawing, colouring, painting, collage materials. Children can transfer patterns they know from one object to another, or invent new patterns entirely.

Materials   Pens, pencils, chalks, paper, paints, collage materials, scissors, glue. Pattern samples, wallpaper, fabrics.

Practical Session   Teacher reads; children read, spell and imagine everyday objects, the classroom, themselves turned to patterns. Some bright, some dull, some big, some small. Imagination can be stretched to ideas beyond themselves and the classroom, e.g. animals, buildings, forests. Children choose to draw, paint, etc., images from imagination. Colour? Size? Shape? Keynote is organization and control of patterns (e.g. 'How might you do this without all the patterns getting mixed up?').

Development   Invention of their own magic spells — language extension, poetry. Function of spell? What changes? Develop using old magazines for pattern sources. Apply to music (magic music-spell?). Drama, plus a combination of art and music. Make masks, objects for the spell, dressing-up materials?

EXAMPLE 12. BRICKWORK

Concepts   Colour, pattern, shape.

Learning Potential Increases awareness of subtle colour-mixes, irregular pattern qualities, shape. Develops colour-mixing and control of medium.

Skills Drawing, colour-mixing, painting.

Stimulus Brickwork outside the school, pictures of brickwork. Discussions, comparisons of colour, shape and pattern.

Options Children find other sources of reference near their homes, prior to session. Teacher brings in old bricks, new bricks. Choice of drawing, painting, or colouring materials.

Materials Small cardboard packages which are collected over a period of time. Light-coloured, brick size or smaller preferred.

Practical Session Children draw brick surface pattern on package (or on paper and glue this before colouring). Paint package carefully mixing colours. When dry, they contribute their brick to a group 'Wall', decorated with 'graffiti' (authorized).

Development Children draw and colour a whole wall. Small individual pictures? Mural? With clay they make small bricks which they texture on the surface to express the idea of 'worn brickwork'? Simple printing using a brick-shaped potato, repeat-printing to construct a building.

EXAMPLE 13. DOODLES INTO PICTURES

Concepts Development/change in drawing.

Learning Potential Fosters ability to invent, imagine and change. Encourages reappraisal of results. Fosters ability to turn 'mistakes' into something else or disguise them.

Skills Drawing, imagining, inventing.

Stimulus Drawing materials.

Option Children exchange doodles with a partner/friend. Stimulus developed to include children responding by doodling to random sounds or stories.

Materials   Paper, pencils, pens, crayons, felt-tips, chalks, paper.

Practical Session   The children doodle on paper first without looking, then by looking and adding to their doodles. Exchange with partner, or keep own doodles and develop them to fit a recognizable shape or become an imaginary creature.

Development   Make collections of doodles over period of time. Use for collage, source of reference for pattern. Copy part of doodle into another design. Assemble doodles into a 'Doodle Mural'. Doodle mobiles?

EXAMPLE 14.   BALANCED SHAPES

Concepts   Balance, awareness of form.

Learning Potential   Develops observation and awareness of balance in shapes, weight, volume. Sense of design in relation to weight.

Skills   Modelling, weighing.

Stimulus   A weighing device, materials, resources for producing abstract shapes (such as a kaleidoscope, polished minerals, pieces of broken bone, fragmented tray-toffee).

Options   Children choose three-dimensional shapes, teacher and children discuss shapes. Use sources of reference for shape, e.g. minerals. Cut in black paper first in two dimensions. Roll modelling material flat? Use clay?

Materials   Weighing balance, scissors, black paper, Plasticine, dough, or clay.

Practical Session   The children look at, talk about, geometric and non-geometric shapes, shapes of stones, mathematical shapes. They try to produce two three-dimensional shapes in Plasticine so that they balance when weighed. Shapes should have some similar characteristic. 'Make me two pebbles with a special shape' is an excellent starting point. Children weigh both shapes and adjust so they balance. Display, discuss.

Development   Weighing, mathematics, cutting black paper shapes which look as if they would balance. Mobiles. Drawing a picture of some shapes being weighed. Joining two shapes together after finding they balance. Making a drawing from the final joined model.

Variety

Each of these ideas can be slightly rearranged to alter the presentation. Variety in presentation often makes the same idea look completely new to children, even if they have done it many times before. There are many occasions, in many areas of the curriculum, when we want to consolidate the same learning. By the time children tumble to the fact that they may previously have done something similar, their work is well under way, and in any case has different aims and a different outcome.

The presentation of ideas can vary principally by making changes to the 'Concepts' and 'Learning Potential' listed here. A project which was designed to encourage awareness of colour might be changed to stimulate awareness of texture or form. Children could be presented with one half of a project this week, and the other half changed for the following week. Alternatively, ideas might be presented in three or four parts during a single art session, or spread across a whole week.

Most of the routes to creative teaching involve choices made from a number of options. In the set examples so far included, it is perfectly possible to reverse the content of two further categories, so that material contained in the 'Development' section, is transferred to that of the 'Practical Session'. We might, for instance, want to change wax-crayon rubbings to a session in which we teach the basic principles and techniques of wax-resist. Plans to work on the concept of 'balance in shapes' might change to 'symmetry in pattern and shape'.

Successful ideas tend to become part of every teacher's repertoire. Yet this has its dangers, especially if we are unable to bring variety into presentation and development. There are already too many artistic clichés for more to be added. Children do enjoy making tissue-paper stained-glass windows, folded paper butterflies and paper snowflakes. But how often are these just done for the sake of interest? How seldom do they form part of a sequenced development? The trouble is that these well-worn clichés are very entertaining. Their popularity is already proven, which makes them irresistible for a teacher who likes a well-mapped, guaranteed, end-product-only approach to art (Chapter 3).

There is no risk, but little possibility of producing anything either unexpected or outstanding.

It ought to be possible to be more creative and generate ideas from an art activity which is already taking place. To achieve this is not as difficult as it seems. Each time there is artwork going on, a strategy which can work is to examine what is happening to see if the following questions produce new ideas for activities.

'Are there skills which need more practice?' (What task? What idea?)

'Do they need more work on pattern?'

'What would happen if we changed the materials?' (Would the ideas change?)

'Is it worth making changes to the activity? Reappraising the presentation?'

'Should they enlarge this?'

'How could we think of this as part of a mural?'

'Is there part of that which needs to be cut out to rescue it? How could it be used?'

A change of medium immediately changes the skills needed to cope with it. The effect is sometimes remarkable. Children who find an idea alien to the materials they are using will often come alive when they try to express it another way. This is not an argument for changing media just for the effect. The point here is that children occasionally become stuck in their expression if they have very little chance to use different media.

All these activities are the source of further learning if we allow them to be. There is, however, no point in assuming children have appropriate skills unless they have already learned them. Whilst art is not simply to teach skills, there are still many practice activities which are necessary for children to learn how to control materials. The keynote is learning, and without much effort on our part it should be possible to think of practice activities which develop control of media. Examples are activities which include skills like mixing paint, using a brush, smoothing a clay surface, or controlling adhesives. Children already have imagination, but we need to give them the psychological 'space' and freedom to use it even within a simple skill. That, and the ability to tie in art activities with children's previous learning, should make art teaching as demanding as any other aspect of education.

9

Using Paint

'No teacher or child in my school ever uses ready-mixed paint.'

(First school headteacher)

'We always use ready-mixed paint.'

(First school headteacher)

THESE TWO opposing views sum up the diverse positions teachers sometimes take up when they want to use paints. There can be established camps and occasionally a no-man's land where the cry is

'We don't use paint here because it's too messy.'

Messy it may be, but the rewards for organizing painting effectively are not to be missed. Most teachers will put up with difficulties if they feel the end results are worthwhile, but it must also be pointed out that there are teachers who dislike using powder colours, block colours, or water colours. So do a few children. To enforce any one particular method of using paint would not be profitable. Yet the advantages of one way over another need examining, not least to show how versatile the medium is.

Very young children may draw what they know, but it is said that they paint what they feel. Quite whether or not that is true is arguable. Their paintings often tend to look strong in feeling or emotion, perhaps because of the fluid nature of the medium, perhaps because that is how they respond to it. Certainly paint offers them expressive characteristics and qualities which no other medium can quite match.

Painting is so fundamental that no art education is complete without some experience of it. Children generally enjoy painting, partly because paint is an unpredictable medium, one full of surprises. For them it has the excitement created by moving areas of wet colour around and across the paper. They can fill shapes, push pigment about and watch the immediate effects created by their brush. Paint is a deceptively easy medium to use, yet it takes years to control and master. It can defy control to the last. However experienced we are in using paint there is always some way of using it which we have not yet come across, and this is one of its great attractions. Of course, how we use it with children seriously affects the outcome of what they do, a factor which can make apparently well-worn subjects like using paint worth closer scrutiny.

Mixing Paints

A child's first experience of paint may be 'finger-painting' where the excitement is more in the doing. Naturally, the results are of limited artistic value. The paints are mixed round and round but not much skill in handling paint is demonstrated. In the nursery, and sometimes in a reception class, children may need to use paints which have already been mixed up for them so that the consistency is thick enough not to run down the paper. When they try out paints with brushes, we can expect them just to dip in a readily available pot and make their exploratory marks. We can expect that, but it is surprising just what children can manage by themselves even at the age of 5 years.

> When I first came to this school I found an incredible resistance to the idea that children could mix their own paints. You really have to demonstrate how to mix up powder paints on a palette so teachers can see. Then they can try it with the children. I put a couple of generous drops of water on a dry enamel plate and wipe the brush on the side of the water pot. Then I dip the wet brush into powder paint, mixing more powder into the drops of water until I can tip up the plate and nothing runs down. The dry powder sticks to the brush. Children soon get the hang of it ... they test their mix by tipping up the plate, but not for long ... really it doesn't take much practice before they know how thick it should be.
>
> (First school headteacher)

Some of the organizational problems have already been mentioned (Chapter 6) but there is no doubt that the availability of water and sinks obviously affects what can be done. The teacher (Chapter 6) who was working under difficulties had eighteen different mixtures of ready-mixed colours for the children to use. But even so she felt that was not enough. Whenever she could, she had her children mixing powder colours together on palettes or enamelled plates. The children were not only mixing powder into a liquid paint, but they were also mixing colours of their own from the ingredients they had.

Where ready-mixed paints are the only ones available, children can still try out mixtures of colour in plastic containers, cooking trays, tin lids, or on laminate surfaces, a little paint at a time to see what happens. They will soon mix them to muddy colours, but that is an important teaching point. Children need to find out what colours do when they are mixed together, even if this is only at the bottom of a used margarine container or a yoghurt pot.

A question that arises is why there should be any rush to teach children to mix their own paints. Surely there is time enough when they are older? There is, but the difference in results between children being independent in their mixing of paint, or dependent on an adult, is staggering. They can have at their disposal a vast range of colour combinations once they are not restricted by using ready-mixed colour. Besides this, we can see that a project such as 'Multi-Coloured Spaghetti' (Chapter 8, Plate 17) is one which is almost impossible to carry out with ready-mixed, thin and diluted paints. The paint needs a certain thick consistency if one colour is not to flood into others, and it should be mixed with other colours for desirable learning to take place.

What a disappointing experience it can be for children always to have to work with thin ready-mixed powder paint on computer paper. Sometimes these thin mixes are made by an adult at the beginning of the week and often seem to become progressively further diluted as the week nears its end. Well-mixed paint, thick enough to obliterate print on newspaper, is by contrast a joy to use. It dries more quickly, produces stronger colours and does not leave the paper in a soggy condition. In contrast, there are paints which are manufactured expressly so they can be used thinly, but their use is quite different. Powder paint as a general rule needs to be mixed thickly, but paints like Cromar, water-colour blocks and the Berol Colour Workshop can be used in gradations, some of them from thick paint to a more watery mix. This is because their dyes are strong enough to allow diluted colour to remain bright. Naturally, it is worth experimenting to find out which paints are versatile and which need to be mixed a certain way. Different consistencies will allow for changes in painting activities and give children experience of a variety of techniques.

As a general rule, where thin mixes are used, a pale or white paper is necessary, though painting thinly on dark papers can have limited attractions. A range of activities which are based on using various consistencies can include

using colour washes

wetting the paper and allowing colour to run down

applying paint with a blunt knife or fingers

drawing with thin paint and filling in shapes with thicker paint

allowing paint to dry, then applying thick paint, pen, pencil, crayon, chalks, or collage materials

experimenting with different mixes and later using the dried end-products for collage.

Colour-Mixing

Of all the characteristics of artwork displayed in any school, colour-mixing is perhaps the most striking. Where children have been limited to using raw primary red, yellow and blue (additionally with green, black and brown as extra colours), the artwork looks remarkably similar and far less personal. It is a disappointment to walk into some schools and see that children have never had the opportunity to mix any colours together themselves. The artwork is trapped in a clash of reds, blues, yellows, oranges and greens without a more subtle shade in sight.

Sometimes there is a particular quality of colour missing (usually a red where only one dark red has been ordered) from the school requisition. This gives a further restricted and impoverished colour range. Even for making the most basic of colour-mixes we will need

(1)   two different reds: a crimson (dark red) and a vermilion (scarlet or bright orange-red)

(2)   two blues: an ultramarine (or royal, bright blue) and a prussian blue (dark blue with a hint of green-black in it)

(3)   two yellows: a chrome yellow (bright yellow) and a yellow ochre (earthy dark yellow).

(4)   black, white.

This range is very austere but ideal for learning how to mix colours. Additionally, brown, purple, orange and green can be ordered. These give greater variety to the shades which can be mixed, but their introduction at an early stage of colour-mixing is questionable. The austere primaries are a restricted minimum for learning about such colours as green and discovering how they might be mixed.

Quite a productive time can be had mixing paints together and never transferring them to paper. It is remarkable how absorbed some children become as they watch colours change on their mixing-plate or palette. There is a stage at which they need to try this and may sometimes learn just as much about colour on the palette as they do using it on their paper.

To have some choice of brushes and paints is equally important. Obviously, not all children want to work with large hog-haired brushes. Some are much happier working on a smaller scale with tiny brushstrokes. The point is made here because there is a tendency to provide thick, hard-wearing, hog-haired brushes as the only ones. More than anything else, children need to experiment with scale, paints, brushes, mixtures and arrangements of materials to find out how they function. The small neat drawings children do are hardly ever appropriate for a hog-haired brush charged with colour. Many children realize this but do not know what the alternatives are. They want to paint their drawing but have previously experienced ruining it through filling in with colour, so they put off the moment when they might have to paint.

Drawing something to 'fill in' initially may make children feel confident, but it soon creates problems, especially if they draw in pencil and then try to colour in their tiny shapes. To solve this problem we can encourage them to draw in chalk or paint, without first doing a detailed drawing. Alternatively, some children may prefer to do a quick preliminary drawing, which they then transfer to a larger scale using chalks. This gives them a good source of reference and confidence since they have already begun to design their painting. If they do work this way, it is well worth suggesting they make their own changes to the design when it is on a grander scale. Children often become frustrated if they cannot quite copy their original sketch exactly and they may need to be taught the value of changing things as they go along.

The effect of paint on white paper and on neutral or grey sugar paper is quite different. Where children are trying to cover the whole paper with paint, white paper is often very difficult to use. It tends to show small pinpricks of bright white when almost all the paper is covered. This is, of course, unless thin water colour is being used. (A feature of using water colour is that it allows for thin translucent washes to build up on the paper.) These pinpricks, where the paint has missed, are less noticeable with grey sugar paper, but children must mix the paint thickly enough to cover the grey. The additional advantage of grey, brown and black papers is that children have the chance to include white paint. (A natural tendency is to mix colours which are darker than the grey paper that children use. Quite a breakthrough in understanding occurs when they find mixtures which are lighter than their paper.

To teach colour theory is not appropriate with young children, especially the 5 year-old, who uses any colour he pleases rather than the expected colouring of things as we know them (Chapter 4). We should not attempt to teach taste in colour, which is associated with personal preference rather than a sensitivity to colour. A good starting point is to have children work on newspaper, putting down dabs or patches of colour to try out their mixing skills. Practising on newspaper is not intimidating for children and it is inexpensive. For added variety, children can use scraps of shaped pieces of paper, half-circles or triangles, for instance, in which they can organize colour and pattern. Painting with a very restricted range of colour (for example, mixing different shades of red) is another worthwhile introduction to discovering their own mixtures.

To minimize the possible mess, at the beginning of learning these skills, it is often as well to start by giving children simple projects such as

finding out about dark colours (for which they could manage with two shades of blue, a black and a red)

finding out about light colours (white, two shades of yellow, and orange)

finding out what two different reds and a black will make

finding out what happens with two different blues and two yellows.

This can be followed by working on colour themes or subjects which particularly lend themselves to further development. The pattern which evolves from patches painted on newspaper, for instance, can become more ordered or complex. Children could paint 'Our Special Red Patterns', 'Our Green Patterns', or 'Our Blue Stripes and Circles'. Or there are subject themes like 'The Red Balloon', 'Fires', 'The Big Red Bus', 'Disco Lights', 'Caves', 'Snow', 'Autumn Colours', or 'Camouflage'.

Colour is sometimes associated with emotion. An emotional response to colour is so personal that we cannot easily begin to analyse it, nor should we. Children can still try out colour-mixes associated with their feelings, but if they do, it is not for us to say what colour is supposed to fit which emotion. We can, however, ask children about their feeling-response to what they paint. Emotional subjects which appeal can often be quickly committed to newspaper or scrap paper, or even painted on a large scale. For example, children can put down patches of colour using a large hog-haired brush (no drawing) inspired by feelings which express

colours of anger
colours of sadness
colours of loud noises
colours of silence
colours of a frightening storm
colours of a sunny day
colours of a day at the seaside.

Opportunities for using paint can also occur very spontaneously. A feature of using paint is that the world itself can actually begin to look more painterly. A cherry tree in full blossom outside the classroom may for some child suggest brushstrokes of pink and white paint. Subjects like 'A Flurry of Snowflakes' or 'The Sunshine on Water' are useful sources of inspiration. In the imagination, subjects like 'Field with a Thousand Greens' or 'A Marmalade Sky' can similarly suggest varieties of colour to paint.

A valuable teaching device is to persuade children to choose and to change, each activity promoting inevitable learning experiences. Two obvious key questions can make children think in this way about what they are painting:

'What are you going to choose?', and
'How are you going to change it?'

Whilst children do not need to change things *at all costs*, without changes and choices their painting can become very fixed and predictable. Choosing and changing gives back responsibility to them for their decisions. The session on colour-mixing may have been inspired by the teacher, but now it is the turn of the pupils to take the initiative and develop their own painting style.

Of course, self-responsibility includes looking after painting materials. Often it is far too easy to create a mess with paint, and unless checked, children will find that to go off and wash palettes, or paint each other, can be more fun than working on the painting. When children first colour-mix, they need practice in looking after paints so that the brush, the water pot, and they themselves stay clean enough to work. Without practice and insistence on care by their teacher, the colours they produce are entirely conditioned by the filthy state of water pots and brushes. Without further encouragement they are likely to clean up inefficiently and painting as an activity can become an experience which is not willingly repeated.

Simple and practical skills which children need to acquire must include mixing bright and light colours whilst the water is clean, making sure brushes are kept reasonably clean, and adding colour to white, rather than the other way round. Beyond these three basics are refinements in the quantities, consistency, variety and organization of painting materials. Teaching children to use paint requires effort and sound organizational skill precisely because it is not a straightforward medium to control. But it offers children such a wide range of effects in comparison, for instance, with drawing. Where drawing may be the string quartet of art, the richness of painting is nearer to being a symphony. Once children become skilful at using paints, their scope for producing expressive work can expand considerably. They have within their grasp the means to colour, eliminate, rearrange and add to the vast array of visual ideas which absorb them.

10

Sequencing Printmaking

IT IS often not long after starting school that children return home with a familiar request to turn up the following day with a potato. Parents may guess what is about to happen. They have seen it all before when they were at school themselves. The idea was to use half the potato on which they made a pattern with a pair of scissors or a blunt knife. Then they printed with it for a time, and if the results were not too messy they displayed them at school or brought them home. Sometimes the potato was pressed on sponges charged with paint, sometimes it was loaded with a brush. Mostly, the activity was a novel afternoon's experience which did not develop much further.

Two distinct paths of development are possible and both of these imply a sequence. That is to say, the work which is done is not simply an afternoon's activity, but bears some relation to what happens before and after it. Either simple printmaking can develop from something else, such as a theme which is already under way, or we can begin at the very beginning and develop a sequence from the first printed marks children make. Along the first path, printing can also grow from rubbings children make, or from embossed wallpaper collages which they cover with a sheet of paper and rub over with crayon. Printmaking, in any case, is a natural development from looking at surfaces and already uses the qualities of a raised surface for its images. Sometimes a professional printmaker will rub over a wood or lino block to see what it looks like.

The two techniques, printmaking and taking rubbings, have obvious similarities.

Alternatively, a second path of development can grow from trying out very simple printing techniques to find out where they lead. A well-known one is to take prints from finger painting (where the teacher takes a print from a laminate surface on which a child has enjoyed pushing paint about). Another technique children may have experienced is using a printing roller and water-based inks to roll over a leaf or a paper stencil. Whatever the elementary experience of printmaking, there comes a point at which children need to explore the technique more fully. For that there must be a different plan of campaign.

The very youngest end of the age-range needs first to try out simple printing activities with very limited materials. Reception children enjoy ready-to-use materials so that they can press an object into paint and quickly transfer it to paper. For them the excitement is immediate and only the forerunner of what can eventually be a rich and expressive medium.

To anyone unused to looking at pre-school and infant art, the first attempts to print or paint may appear to be superficial and chaotic. However, this takes no account of the fact that there is a sequence of development to any artistic learning which (as has already been pointed out in Chapter 8) begins with exploration and play. The rhythmic stamping of a bottle top, a lid, or a potato on newspaper, is just as important to the learning sequence as is refined and careful placing of one printed shape next to another. At this young age, not much consideration of where the bottle top might be placed can be expected, nor is there generally a deliberate choice of colour.

Bottle tops, scraps of polystyrene, cotton reels, junk and vegetables are all ideal surfaces for elementary printmaking. For the beginner, printmaking can be organized with plastic margarine containers lined with sponge or rag. These serve as ideal reservoirs for paint and are not messy. If there are enough interesting mixes of colour available, children can produce excellent results by using them as a stamping-pad. Enough sponge-filled containers and a variety of objects for printing make for a successful combination, though very young children may need to have their potato cut to a shape they can more easily hold. The first experience of printmaking is novel and short-lived and, so long as all the materials are to hand, it can be enjoyable and educationally worthwhile.

. Younger children may like these unsophisticated encounters with printmaking but we must consider how a sequence of learning develops from here. What steps can we take to push development well beyond that of novelty and entertainment?

If children are going to progress further than a 'press-and-print' approach we must take account of acquired skills like colour-mixing (Chapter 9). Obviously there is a considerable difference in the range of colours and techniques which is possible when children can already handle colour-mixing. A whole new experience opens up. From colour-mixing activities, children can develop more ambitious organization of their materials. Their workspace can be arranged so that they can charge a printing surface with a drip-free mixture of their own making and not let paint splash all over the place. Printmaking, using margarine containers as a reservoir, can be abandoned in favour of a far wider range of colours and tones.

A crucial aspect of sequencing is to devise games which teach skill in printing before any specific subject matter is introduced. One such exercise is to see how many times a potato can be printed on scrap paper or newspaper before the effect cannot be seen. Many children assume that a potato must be fully charged with colour each time they put it down on paper. Most of them will put far too much paint on their potato when they first start. Yet the mottled printed pattern of a potato surface can be attractive and add character to the design. To help understand this, children who have not quite got the message can try using a piece of newspaper as a preliminary blotter for the potato so that they only ever print the second pressing on their final designs. Or they can usefully be in competition with each other to see who can print with the least amount of paint on their potato.

Another valuable skill-teaching idea is to try to have them printing by pressing as lightly as they possibly can to see the effect. Children seem to have no difficulty whatever pressing down hard and to print lightly seems quite alien to their natural inclinations. It is surprising how much more care they will actually take once they try out these competitive learning activities.

The plan of campaign could also include cutting a variety of usable shapes from potatoes, wood blocks and ready-to-hand objects for printing. Initially, children do not then have to cope with the problem of cutting anything for themselves. The reason for removing this problem is to deal with other issues and for children to learn printing rather than cutting skills. It is perfectly possible to practise printing by dividing up a potato into chips rather than using the familiar halved shape. The activity can extend throughout a whole week and cost very little. Later,

Figure 25   Text Blocks. Age 8. 300 x 400 mm

wallpaper scrapers can be used for cutting a flat printing surface on a vegetable. There are also blunt knives, potato peelers, shaped wooden spatulas, or inverted pen nibs (in holders), which are all useful cutting tools for making patterns. Twigs with an end cut and shaped like a glue spreader make simple and safe cutting knives. Blocks of potato which have a triangular-shaped printing surface, pieces shaped like cake slices, rectangular, square and curved shapes, all add to a miscellany of chippings.

An example of an activity designed to develop printing skills is seen in Figure 25. Here children begin by printing shapes next to a block of newspaper text or advertising matter. Shapes and colours can be limited so they concentrate on placing their marks carefully. An important teaching point is for children to learn to follow their own intentions. That is to say, they need sometimes to be able to draw a guideline and carefully print their potato next to it, making sure they closely match their potato edge to the line they drew. Some practice in placing printed shapes of potato edge to edge, point to point, or on a curved line (Figure 26), is also excellent as an additional way of developing this skill.

Drawing ruled lines at different angles, drawing around objects and creating meandering lines, all are variations of this practice activity. With each simple project children will usually learn a fraction more control. Some surprising patterns can be discovered and there is often a very rewarding development of skill evident for use in future work. Practice ideas for these activities might be of this kind:

(1) Draw me three lines like snakes across your paper. Choose mixtures of one colour and two shapes, and place them as carefully as you can against the line.

(2) See what pattern you can make with a ruler and pencil. Then add your printed shapes, carefully following your line with the edge of your shape.

(3) Choose two colours and work on squared paper [large squares if possible], carefully deciding where to put your potato printing.

(4) Draw round a dinner-plate and put patterns inside with your potato [or bottle top?] starting from the outside line and working inwards to the middle.

(5) Make a pattern of curved and straight lines. Develop your design using these as a guide.

Figure 26   Curved Line. Age 8. 505 x 387 mm

(6) Put all your potato shapes point to point so that they touch when they print.

(7) Print your potato shapes edge to edge leaving very little or no gap between shapes.

In contrast to this controlled 'drawn line' approach (see also Plates 22, 23, 24) children can work quite freely using no guidelines whatever. An interesting problem to set them, for example, is to begin with a printed shape of their choice, work from the centre of their paper and try to make that central area look more interesting than the outside areas. The children learn a great deal about different ways to emphasize their work through choice of shape, tone, colour and arrangement of design. Emphasis is an important concept, one which has universal recognition in composition and interpretation in all the arts. This particular printmaking activity is one in which children can go on adding small shapes to the centre, so that they overlap each other. It involves decisions about when to stop and how much paper to leave showing, and judgements about its final impact.

A more sophisticated development is to change the shade of colour slightly each time the potato is printed. The printed shapes gradually change in colour from, say, red to orange, or blue to pink. To control such a colour change, especially where subtle colour-mixes are involved, demands skills which are not unusual but are determined by practice. Children may also be able to tackle working from light to dark colours or working with pattern on dark-toned papers (as in Plate 22).

As a variation on pattern, some children may be able to cut a letter of the alphabet on their potato. Even if they could not do this (and most can manage a straight-sided letter), alphabet letters still provide a useful way of producing patterns. The shape of each letter can be a substitute for drawn guidelines and incidentally reinforce children's awareness of letter formation. Patterns can additionally be cut into the potato surface, or round the outside edges, changes which give a different effect from using the potato as an entirely solid shape.

Sooner or later printed shapes will suggest interesting subject matter. Snake-shaped lines will become snakes or caterpillars. Many of these subjects grow naturally from the creation of patterns. Children will sometimes see spirals as shells or snails. The triangular shapes of chopped-up potato may suggest to one child the spines of a prehistoric monster. To another they may be the cogs of a gigantic and futuristic machine.

Putting Ideas to the Test

The purpose in presenting the following ideas in this particular format is to encourage some flexibility of approach. Most educational ideas are changed by the best of teachers. Yet it is worth knowing that there are two distinct ways of doing this, each of which has a very different outcome. One way seems to be to extract only a fraction of surface level material from the ideas as they are presented. This strategy is one which can make the most excellent of schemes, maths, art, or language, fail miserably. The end result is a diluted version of the original. A better approach is to adapt and add to what is already there whilst retaining the principles of the idea. Some ideas which do not initially appeal may then serve to spark off others.

In the first example, which follows, some indication of learning potential is shown. From there onwards the whole emphasis of projects must be decided by the teacher in the light of the principles, concepts and learning potential outlined in previous chapters.

THREE KINGS

Learning potential includes colour-mixing, printing, sticking, language development, judgement of shape and designing.

This can begin with colour-mixing skills. Working in small groups, the children follow this by making patterns with potato prints on strips of paper, about 500 mm x 70 mm. This includes using black paper strips with white shapes printed by the children. These are then discussed as if they are lapels, or trimmings for an ornate and jewelled costume. After discussion, working on scrap paper, the children design for a large-scale costumed king which they draw out and print with various objects. They might print jewelled braid effects on black paper, cut them and collage with extra pieces of printed pattern, paper doilies and gold foil. There are options available to the teacher to vary materials, or limit them, allow choice, change scale and make a mural.

CASTLES AND HOUSES

Teacher or children cut a potato into a useful block or brick shape. Children then discuss with their teacher castles, houses, windows, doors, moats and building techniques. The teacher also provides resources, books, visual aids. The potato block is used as a printing brick/stone for designing castles and houses. This technique has similarities with children's previous experience of using wooden building blocks, Lego and construction equipment. The project can be developed into three-dimensional work with model-making a useful outcome. Children print on cardboard boxes and assemble them. The scale of these can be large enough for the boxes to become a model which can be temporarily inhabited or used for drama.

SPACESHIPS

This printmaking theme is tackled using black paper and printing in white. (Reference can be made to the 'Black and White' project in Chapter 8.) The children draw out, in rough, spaceships, planets, spacemen. The teaching points arise from the difficulties of mixing whites, greys, light colours. Developments for teaching could include specific projects on space travel, murals, displays for the hall or corridor areas. Joint efforts can be assembled, collaged.

GARDENS

A possibility here is to study petal shapes and leaf shapes. Printing may be done either on dark or light papers (or both) with obviously different results. Instead of producing a solitary flower or plant, children can develop ideas by printing over shapes until the garden contains a profusion of their own designs. Ideas: 'A Multi-Coloured Flower Bed', 'The Giant Leaf Plant', 'Repeated Leaf Shapes'.

MACHINES

This project can grow from printing with bottle tops and lids. The children begin to invent machines which are meant to perform functions. Fantasy: 'The Fastest Machine', 'The Wheely Machine', 'The Football Machine'. Reality: 'Bus', 'Car', 'Railways', 'Farm Machinery'.

MURALS

Murals can develop from any of the projects mentioned, but sometimes it is worth having a 'Pattern Mural' on which all the children print in turns. The organization of this, rationing of space, themes and decisions, makes for a productive learning experience. Such subjects as 'A Stripe Mural', 'Curves and Lines', 'Sponge Print Mural', can be developed as works in their own right.

CIRCLE SEGMENTS

Instead of children filling circles with pattern, this time they draw segments. Alternatively, they may incorporate ideas from mathematics. The aim is to use pattern which follows the design of a segment. This simple process allows for great variety in use of colour and shape inside each segment. For example, small triangular chips of potato can be used as the sole interior printed shape, or there might be a variety of different shapes. Colours can be limited to two or three, or children choose from a wider range.

THE SUN

There are various ways to develop this. Stories of 'Sun Gods', pictures of the sun, and fantasy songs, poems, rhymes and anecdotes provide a stimulus. A considerable variety of shapes and colour-mixes can be tried (an aim might be to build up a rich surface by overlapping shapes). The scale of the 'Sun' pictures is important. Imagine, for instance, two or three children printing a large sun shape on a mural. Developments include 'Sun and Clouds', 'Sun and Shadows', 'Sun and Rain', 'Hot Pictures' (fantasy).

BIRDS

As with many other creatures, the theme of birds allows children to print shapes instead of painting with a brush. Many children find they have much more confidence using printed shapes for feathers than they do brush drawing. A development might be to print from real feathers using water-based inks and a roller. An advantage of themes such as 'Birds' or 'Fish' is that they may require very little drawing ability in the first instance. As a consequence they can often lead children to observe more closely and develop more sophisticated drawing skills.

FIREWORKS

This subject is very successful even with very young children, especially if they can use thickly mixed whites, yellows, oranges and colours associated with fireworks. On black sugar paper, the children can try out their printing with much more freedom than, for example, the 'Spaceship' project demanded. Here, they have the chance to let fantasy run riot as they create brightly toned mixtures for a firework display.

Three-Dimensional Prints

Some of the patterns children produce make exceptionally good three-dimensional designs. Prints can be cut up and reassembled into sculpture. A finished print can be displayed as a cylinder, or the cylinder used as a Christmas decoration. Printing can be effective on masks and paper costumes. Children can design these working from skirt shapes, dress shapes, boxes, cones and shapes used for mobiles. The prints need not necessarily be large or elaborate.

There is an endless number of art activities which can have a carefully considered sequence. The more rigid the sequence, however, the more difficult it is to allow for children's differing work rates and this needs to be taken into account when organizing sessions. Sequencing should be sufficiently flexible to allow for individual differences. There is little point forcing children to jump through tightly organized artistic hoops under the assumption that they will eventually learn something useful. There are broader categories for a sequenced learning programme.

So far, the sequence described has been mapped out so that children develop ideas through

(1) play, rhythmic stamping of bottle tops, lids
(2) experience of colour-mixing
(3) simple practice games on newspaper (pressing objects as lightly as possible, printing until no effect is seen)
(4) controlled pattern, choices of colour, shape, drawn lines
(5) development of subject matter
(6) large-scale projects, murals, three-dimensional work.

This is a useful but not sacrosanct sequence. Large-scale work is not, after all, the final objective for all printmaking projects. It is different rather than better. Of much greater importance is the development of a sequence of learning which arises in response to what children do. Such a sequence is likely to evolve as we ask,

'Do they need more practice in cutting?'

Figures 27, 28   Parrot, Boat. Age 8. 330 x 450 mm, 390 x 310 mm

'Do they need to have a break from this and do some colour-mixing?'
'How can they cope with printing in artwork connected with the theme
of ... ?'
'Could the work they're already doing be developed to include ... ?'
'What might that tree bark look like printed instead of painted?'

It would be a great mistake repeatedly to practise skills until only the
technical side of things was perfect. Children need to try out ambitious
ideas for subject matter in the sequence, as well as to improve their
technical skills. Rather in the way handwriting skills can still develop
when children are inventing their own stories, colour-mixing or printing
skills can be developed through other imaginative pieces of work.
Sequencing any activities demands professional judgement especially
when deciding what to leave out as well as what to put in. No sequence
which is formulated in advance is ever going to replace a teacher's
evolving sequence in response to the children's progress. If we want to
develop printmaking to some depth and use it as a way of developing a
wide variety of artistic skills, sequencing cannot be ignored as a crucial
element of the process.

129

11

Collage and 3-D

THE MEDIUM of collage can be described as a recipe for visual confusion. This is because without careful control of abundant colour and pattern, the results of cutting, tearing and sticking things down tend to look jumbled and disorganized. The best collages, by contrast, show considerable skill in sorting materials and making them work together. If children thoughtlessly assemble anything that takes their fancy, the effect is to blur their designs, rather than organize them with clarity. Handled well, collage is a richly individual medium for designing. The main advantage of the technique is that materials can be tried out and moved around before being stuck down. The artist can put off the decision to finalize things until satisfied with the arrangement.

Collage has similarities with sorting activities. Children are often asked to sort numbers, colours, beads and blocks. If we take it as a teaching principle that activities should be sequenced (Chapter 10), there is every good reason why sorting collage materials could be used to this end. The opportunities for developing visual discrimination are limitless. Children can sort similar patterns or textures. They can sort colours, lines, different printed typefaces, fabrics, threads, foils, leather, metal, feathers, fur, grasses, or seeds. All this before they start to produce anything creative.

At the younger end of the age-range, children particularly enjoy tearing shapes from paper, rather than cutting them. They also enjoy finding things which have different tactile qualities, like rough, smooth, rounded, or flat surfaces. The opportunity here for language development from these tactile experiences is an obvious one. Besides this, very little imagination is needed to devise practical maths tasks using various collage materials. Sets of five seeds and five lids, four blue wools and six black, three silver papers and seven sweet wrappers, could aid the teaching of number. Additionally, maths games where one colour represents a particular number can help to combine and support these different areas of the curriculum.

So long as children do not become totally bored by extra sorting activities, they can build up a useful resource for collages. A demanding but extremely worthwhile activity is to begin by sorting scraps of torn newspaper, a few centimetres square, into three different piles. One pile could be scraps of headlines with large letter shapes. Another could have parts of photographs and the remaining collection could be of small-sized text. It is quite surprising how interesting an effect the use of this simple resource has in a collage where there are bright colours. Even on its own, to use three tones of newspaper collage can be very attractive and a welcome change from screwed-up pieces of coloured tissue paper.

Scissor-cutting skills are just as important as tearing paper, and awareness of shape can be encouraged by cutting repeated units. For instance, children can cut shapes which represent fish scales, or feathers, and carefully use them as units to build up their own designs of fishes or birds. It is well worth encouraging children to choose how they themselves will limit materials so that the collages have some character. Could they, for example, work using newspaper only? Or could they limit themselves to two or three colours? Might they work with the same repeated shape?

When one design feature of a collage is very strong, it will often support a wide variety of colours and textures. Supposing children were to cut small brick-shaped rectangles from a varied range of colours and patterns. These they might assemble to make a richly patterned wall or building. Ordinarily, a multi-coloured design could look confused and over-fussy. But choosing such a simple shape as a rectangular brick binds the design together. It imposes its own unity and limitations of shape.

The repeated shape idea could easily be developed in other ways, taking titles such as 'Marbles', 'Beach Balls', 'Trees', 'Clouds', 'Fencing', 'Paving Slabs', Petals', or 'Patchwork'. In fact, from repeated shapes a whole theme could emerge. Imagine generating ideas around a theme of 'Sweets and Sweet Jars'. The theme could cover a spectrum of visual ideas from a 'Design for a Sweet Shop' (based on reality) to 'The Biggest Lollipop in the World' (fantasy). An additional development is to use different materials besides paper and to work in media other than collage, like paint and crayon.

Children accustomed to choosing what medium to use can bring a great deal of their own originality to each theme. As far as the teacher is concerned, the effort needed to develop ideas diminishes as pupils offer more. It also lessens with continual practice in thinking around possible themes. In fact, five minutes spent scribbling ideas on the back of an envelope can sometimes create the beginnings of enough useful work for days (see also Chapter 5).

The concept of 'contrast' in collage is an important one but not easily taught or understood. Most muddled collages we see are confused because one material merges into another. Sometimes this is because the shape is rather ambiguous, more often it happens because dark material has not been contrasted with light. Colour has not contrasted with colour, pattern has not found a place next to a plain area. Of course, more sophisticated adult collages work well without contrast, yet for children who have little control of the medium, contrast is a concept which they put to good use. They can develop awareness of it in any number of ways. They benefit from comparing the effect of sticking dark paper shapes over light ones, or light over dark. They can also try to discover which colours and shapes might stand out against each other, which ones tend to lack contrast. And they can compare strong patterns with subtle, large with small, brightly coloured with dull.

Many collage materials, like leather and fabric, are difficult for children to use. Leather does not cut sufficiently easily to create a clear and readable shape, so contrast of colour and tone is vital as an alternative way of making the work more readable to the eye. With the best of intentions, a number of teachers produce murals or friezes which are collaged without any regard for this concept of contrast. The same colours or tones are often used for both background and foreground, where with some thought they could be much more decisive as design features.

A simple guide to avoid confused images is to keep specific colours and patterns for different objects in the collage. A particular blue might be used solely for part of the sky and other blues reserved for objects elsewhere in the collage. Similarly, patterns can be representative of only one element, like vegetation or building materials. In fact part of the all-important decision-making process is to sort out which material suits the particular part of the content. Is black and white newspaper the best choice for that elephant? Should we save the red for this wooden fence?

Many of the drawings and photographs we see in books depict objects in their most easily readable view. Usually this is a side view or a silhouette which has an outline or edge which conveys the maximum information. In such a complicated medium as collage, silhouette shapes are helpful ingredients. That is not to say that the side-view silhouette is the best, simply that it is readable. Children will need to spend time finding out just what a silhouette is, or play with positive and negative shapes from the same piece of black paper to see what the effect of maximum contrast is.

Obviously whenever a shape is cut from black paper it leaves its negative in the remainder. Both positive black paper and negative space can be incorporated into a design. Picasso, Braque and, notably, Schwitters were artists who found that pieces they had left over from cutting out were fascinating resources for collage. Naturally, there is a unifying link between the cut shape and its waste surround, so it is not surprising that artists found using both was visually appealing.

Children may well discover that the assorted junk they collect themselves has strong visual attractions. Part of the learning experience is for them to collect their own collage materials and bring them into the classroom. Storage difficulties apart, the collections they make often provide a good talking point as well as being a cheap art material. Needless to say, teachers of this young age-range, 4−9 years, become great hoarders of all sorts of material for collage. Practically anything which will stick down is worth collecting.

For most purposes, school glue, PVA, or even paste (so long as it has no fungicide) will do for sticking collage. Occasionally, some stronger tube adhesives may be necessary under the teacher's supervision. A useful organizational device is to have children gluing on magazines so they can turn the page when the surface becomes too messy. Glue does seem to travel in the hands of inexperienced children and some skill in instructing children how to use it is called for. If about a centimetre depth is put in the bottom of a pot, the glue is less likely to travel up the spreader. At its messiest moments, collage is a great test of skill in handling materials. Children and their teachers discover what will stick and what refuses to do so. Where there are problems these usually involve too much glue, or the wrong kind for the job.

Rounded surfaces, such as cardboard rolls, and curved junk refuse to stick easily, as do plastic containers and heavily waxed surfaces. The choice open is to use ingenious combinations of tabs, staples, strong glues and adhesive tape, or take a wise step and avoid curve against curve. A hot-glue gun is a possibility as it will stick almost anything but this would not be safe for children to use themselves. There is really no such thing as failure in collage because it is all about techniques of assembling what we can. A child who discovers something is impossible to stick with the glue being used may learn as much about technical problems as can be learned about art. The experience may not be very enjoyable but still educationally worthwhile.

Every so often, children will ask if they can add paint to their collage. This is usually an afterthought but it can also be tried quite deliberately as a starting point. From this beginning comes the combination of drawing and collage, or paint and collage, both of which are as valid as collage is in its own right. Coloured chalks, ink and felt-tipped pens can all add to the work. Particularly useful are chalk and ink which can add to and emphasize a collaged shape. Paint, if it is thick enough, can obliterate confused parts of a collage and unify it. In some adult artists' collages, where three-dimensional blocks of wood are stuck to a flat surface, it is not unusual to find the whole work has been painted in matt white paint. The shapes used were probably painted white because they needed some unifying element.

Many paintings which incorporate collage never began that way. The artist has arrived at the collage through a process of change and may even have rescued the work by incorporating collage. Sometimes in the classroom, a pattern-making session which went wrong can lend itself to a rescue operation. Instead of the results being thrown away, they can be cut up later and glued down again on another paper surface, the materials used and reused.

Assemblages

We usually think of collage as being flat and two-dimensional in comparison with sculpture. But it becomes three-dimensional as what might be called 'assemblage'. The term is self-explanatory. Scrap materials are assembled into three-dimensional forms. These may well represent a fantasy creature or become interesting objects in their own right. Once the concept has been introduced that forms can exist independently of subject matter, children enjoy making them to see what they can produce. The assemblage no longer has to 'be' something recognizable. Children are far less worried by the abstract than adults seem to be.

Figure 29 Paper Strip Sculpture. Age 8.

A number of remarkable assemblages can be produced by working on themes like 'Balance', 'Symmetry', or 'Tall Shapes'. Again, the use of units, like boxes or cotton reels, paper cups, egg-containers and packing material helps. Simple three-dimensional shapes can be made from paper strips and assembled into larger forms. Paper strips are cheap to produce, can be bent, curved and stuck. Children can devise shapes which they repeat (a good learning activity in its own right) and the variations possible are endless once these units are made. As a development of this idea, children might stick some of their repeated shapes around a paper cylinder or around a box.

Displays of paper-strip sculptures (Figure 29) can prove interesting discussion points. There is a great deal to look at in terms of shape, shadow effects, textures and colour. Ideas may be triggered by

looking at shadows

making a 'Shadow Show' using coloured strips of paper and a light source (choice?)

using black and white

painting the sculptures

making paper-strip mobiles

drawing the paper-strip assemblages

finding different ways to display them

combining sculptures into a very large assemblage.

When cutting skills are well advanced children can use shapes cut from egg-trays as a resource. These are the papier-mâché egg-trays which are thin enough for children to cut. Allowing the scissors to travel until an interesting unit is found produces a very original shape. Some of the units can then be made into creatures, or alternatively they can simply be glued together as three-dimensional forms. Sufficient learning often takes place through the cutting and painting activities which children do. Painted assemblages made from egg-trays are often so striking that their original source material can become cleverly disguised.

Papier mâché, newspaper pulped with paste, is a useful modelling medium. Its chief drawback is that it can take ages to dry out if it is of any thickness. Yet it has its uses, chiefly in producing lightweight forms when applied in layers over a supporting former or frame. Practically any object can be covered with papier mâché and its use is not restricted to the traditional one of covering clay. However, if we want to rescue the underlying former it needs to be smeared with soap or covered initially with wet paper on which there is no paste. An essential consideration is that papier mâché should not take too long to complete. Children become bored with a piece of work which seems to go on for weeks. Although in the past the medium has found its best use in producing puppets and masks, there are many other forms possible. With wire as a former, an alternative is to make large sculptures by building up with paper from the wire to the finished piece.

Puppetry is a subject to which much time could be devoted. Some schools successfully make a feature of it, using it as a centrepiece of their artistic and dramatic output. But in that case the papier-mâché medium is really secondary to the drama and used because it provides a cheap, flexible and lightweight modelling medium. There is a clear link between puppetry, assemblage, collage and papier-mâché techniques involving sticking and using found objects. Many of the decisions taken are similar for each medium. Children can of course use all three media to express dramatic ideas. But they do need to try out rough and ready puppets assembled from a 'bit box' first before they embark on a longer-term papier-mâché model. Decorated socks, paper bags, tubes and card shapes taped to sticks, are some of the simplest ways to begin puppetry.

The keynote here is involvement and more elaborate puppets should arise out of a need created by the children's enthusiasm for drama. The last thing we want to do is dampen their interest by enforced sticking of small pieces of paper, layer upon layer. Far better to make quickly assembled puppets from scrap materials and use them inventively. There are no prizes for beginning any three-dimensional work by devising over-ambitious projects. Very successful puppets can be assembled using oddments like crumpled newspaper and buttons. The more rough and ready they are, the funnier they often appear. The more limited the materials, the more impressive they can sometimes be.

Claywork

Tactile experience with clay offers children qualities no other medium has. Plasticine (also dough made with flour and water) is basically a much easier medium to use for modelling but clay teaches children about quite different properties. Clay becomes tired or hard with working. It dries out, it can be carved when it is leather-hard, it cracks and becomes unusable. It can be reclaimed and used over again and it can be made into a slip (clay and water mixed to a slurry) which is used for joining and decorating. Some children actually like to work with clay. Others initially find it quite unpleasant and feel it is dirty and associate it with garden soil. Clay is in fact a very clean medium, but children need to be encouraged to explore and discover that it is and be taught interesting ways of using it.

Little children, working on a clay table or on an individual board for the first time, may not be expected to produce anything remarkable. They need time to push and pull the clay about, to enjoy its malleable quality and to discover its limitations. A new experience for them may well be to work the clay with their eyes shut. Tactile experience is very different without sight and an important feature of their early development. Later on in their school lives it can be virtually impossible to persuade children to work without looking. Here is an opportunity to discover the nature of a new substance by touch alone and develop discussion about tactile qualities.

Young children generally like modelling with clay but they do need stimulating to make their models interesting. An approach is to discuss movement with children so that they can attempt to put action into their models. They can imagine twisting movements and discover characteristics which make each animal special. The teacher's sensitive questioning is important and can concentrate on specific features like eyes, teeth, or spines. Questions can be asked such as 'What shape is their back?' or 'How fat are they in comparison with … ?'

Clay does not behave as children expect it will. They may need to start off by making models of animals which have sturdy legs so that their animal does not collapse. Anything which looks as if it might crack and fall off should be discussed with the child who constructed it. Clay spikes on a prehistoric monster will drop off, as likely as not, if they are not properly smoothed into the rest of the clay. Structurally, clay spikes may need to be pulled out to pyramid shapes, or cone shapes, to survive when dry. Animals' tails might need to be smoothed into the side so as to avoid knocking them in the dry state. Models with legs may also need to be supported or turned upside down until they are dry enough to stand up without collapsing. It is possible to make a clay support for this if it proves to be particularly difficult to keep the model's shape.

A method for jointing is to 'weld' joints with additional clay rather than use water as a binder. Clay is not difficult to smooth into a joint and once the weld is made, the joint is very strong indeed. Making a joint with water by rubbing the clay to a slip is a process needing some experience, and children usually find it difficult. A teaching point is to explain that although clay will stick together in the plastic state, it falls apart when it is dry unless it is well joined.

Wooden surfaces are excellent for claywork, as are composition floor-tiles. Clay tends to stick to laminate surfaces and it is often easier to have small individual boards so that the clay model need not be moved before it dries out. Usually the clay in its plastic state arrives in a polythene bag. If the bag is not kept cool and closed up, the clay dries very quickly and becomes unusable. Even a bag left open for an hour will not be as good as it should be. A garden spray filled with water is a useful tool for wetting clay which is to be stored, and giving a brief spray inside the bag will help the polythene stick to the clay as the bag is refastened.

Some children working on a table or board produce rather flat, two-dimensional work at first, and will need to pick up a ball of clay and try modelling more freely. A halfway stage between two and three dimensions is to draw into clay or to model from a preliminary drawing. Sooner or later the fact that all sorts of marks can be pressed into clay will be discovered. Children may begin with their fingers but discovering tools and scraps with which to make impressions in clay is all part of learning. These may be used to make clay tiles and in a short time a useful tool-box of mark-making objects can easily be collected.

Early experience with Plasticine is not entirely wasted. Children are used to rolling out snakes and sausage shapes, a primitive skill that can be utilized to make simple coiled pots and models. It is far better to build on their skills than be scornful of them. Practically all the well-known clichés in young children's art can be turned to advantage with a little creative teaching. Snakes and sausages, birds' nests and baskets full of eggs, are common enough. But they can be translated into detailed models which include trees and birds, picnics and plates of various carefully shaped foods, all made from clay.

The surface can be decorated either by impressing shapes in the clay or by adding pieces of clay and welding or smoothing them in. Texture can be added by scratching the clay surface when it is still semi-hard. Once it is dry, to smooth with abrasive tools or to scratch designs is a health hazard. Potters recently have turned to using face masks to avoid inhaling clay dust and on no account should children be faced with this hazard. Dry clay should be carefully monitored and consideration given to its storage to ensure it does not create dust.

Pinching or squeezing lumps of clay into shapes is another well-known modelling technique. The main thing to remember is that if clay is to be fired later, models should be hollow and pierced with a hole to let out gas and air if there is an air pocket. Otherwise they may explode in the kiln (though not if heavily grogged clay is used). If the surface of clay cracks as it is being used children will also need to be shown that the surface can be smoothed over. If the clay does not respond, a damp sponge or rag can be used, or slip applied with a finger or brush. The all too obvious alternative, to provide water with clay, is simply asking for trouble. Some teachers can manage to control its use but all too often children, water and clay mix together with alarming results.

Unless models or simple pots are completed in one art session they will need to be covered to stop them drying out. Wet paper towels, water spray and thin polythene is a solution. It may be that the idea is to let the clay dry to a leather-hard state, dry enough to carve, but not so dry that it can no longer easily be worked. If there is enough storage space in the school, an old discarded fridge is an ideal place for work in progress. A laminate cupboard and polythene is the next best option.

Kiln firings are an exciting transformation of clay into pot or ceramic. Try to find a school which will fire claywork, or alternatively build a home-made sawdust kiln. Sawdust kilns, made with bricks and chicken wire, topped with a metal dustbin lid, are filled with sawdust and clay-work. The kiln is lit from the top and takes about a day and a half to smoulder and vitrify the clay. Providing children understand beforehand that their precious models will emerge blackened, the experience of seeing a sawdust firing under way may be worth the trouble. However, the resulting blackened models are sometimes a shock when they emerge, and cannot very successfully be glazed.

Reclaiming clay which has dried out is easily achieved. The temptation to reclaim dry models which are dear to children's hearts should be resisted but there may be good reasons for reusing dried-out clay. The intention is to reclaim the clay, make it workable and return it to its original plastic state. This job falls to the teacher rather than the children, though a few may be able to help out if they are old enough. With experience, reclaiming clay becomes easier, but it does need some experiment and practice.

Put the dry clay in a plastic bucket which has a lid (or polythene and a rubber band) and put in a small amount of water, checking each day to see if the dry clay has absorbed it. After a day or two the clay will be soft enough to divide up and manipulate on a dry absorbent surface, like wood or plaster. If a plaster slab can be made this is ideal. But it should be remembered that fragments of plaster cause clay to explode in a kiln. Wood may be better for an inexperienced beginner. If the clay is too sticky it can be left for a while to dry out and then pushed about (or 'wedged' as is the technical term). Air holes need to be pushed out of the clay by thumping it on a solid wooden surface and by squeezing and 'wedging'. Sticky clay will eventually become usable by being manipulated even if the initial effort seems unsuccessful.

Some of the clay in the original bag may be a fraction too hard to use. In this case, take a small lump about the size of a tennis ball, hollow it with the thumb and fill it up with water. Leave it upright in a polythene bag for a day, or until the clay has absorbed the water. Then push it about until it becomes soft enough to use again. Rather like making pastry, some trial and error is needed in the early stages of learning how to reclaim clay. Wedging is impossible to describe but no real harm comes from experimenting with clay to see what is possible. Clay called 'crank mixture' is much easier to reclaim than stoneware clay as it absorbs moisture more quickly. It can also be worked by children for a much longer period of time before it becomes difficult to use.

Of all media, clay is the one with which teachers are probably the least familiar. There is much to be gained from learning with the children, as well as finding out through reading specialist books, or attending in-service courses. Glazing and kiln-firing are the two areas needing specialist knowledge, but other teachers are nearly always ready to help and the knowledge needed is not vast by any means. There are glazes available for school use now which are painted on the 'biscuit-fired' pots. It is also possible (with a little experimenting by adding PVA glue) to paint this glaze on the dry clay and fire in a kiln.

Thinking in three dimensions and developing skills in modelling extend the usual range of activities we associate with young children. To think in three dimensions and use three-dimensional media is very different from the more usual ways children work. As adults they may never use clay again but the opportunity to use it should not only be offered to them. It is essential to any art education programme we care to plan.

12

Design and Problem-Solving

OVER THE last few years much discussion has centred on design and problem-solving as worthwhile and necessary activities for children. The Design Council project (1984 onwards), government departments and various teachers' journals have raised the issue of design, particularly in relation to craft and technology. Two clear assumptions are that designing is a good thing and problem-solving a necessary function of everyday life. No one quite agrees on a description of either of these activities. Yet they satisfy the need in some minds for education to have useful vocational outcomes.

In the early years of schooling, design may sound an inappropriate and highly sophisticated area of activity. We tend to think of young children more involved with exploring their first marks on paper and finding out about art materials. Some of them can hardly hold a pencil or manage a pair of scissors, let alone design something. How can we expect them to understand anything about design? How can we expect teachers to introduce design to their children when they themselves may be unsure of what it is?

There are several promising aspects of design and problem-solving to examine, but they need first to be put in perspective. Design is a new facet of art education in the early years. It would be tempting to allow it to displace an otherwise healthy art education programme in schools, and this could well happen (as it already has in one or two secondary schools).

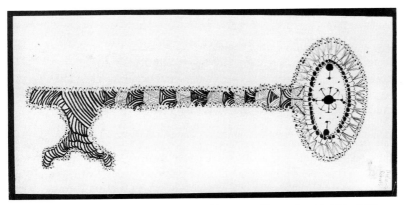

Figure 30 Design for a Key to Open a Treasure Chest. Age 9. 400 x 172 mm

Design and problem-solving are an enrichment of any art education programme, not a substitute for all the other important art activities children do. Arguments will go on about the part design and problem-solving play in the curriculum, but it would be a pity if they were ignored and an even greater pity if they became the only justifiable art for children to experience.

If we assume that problems can be solved and that children should be involved in solving them, a likely effect is for us to applaud not only creativity but initiative, self-responsibility and fitness for purpose. It would be difficult to argue against children becoming design-conscious or taking responsibility for solving their own problems. Self-responsibility has, after all, been encouraged over the last century in many of our schools. We want children to consider problems, generate new ideas and develop a wide range of alternative solutions for themselves. Without our deliberately involving them in design and problem-solving processes at school they are less likely to encounter strategies for doing this and less likely to give their creativity vocational relevance.

Children have the capacity to live in fantasy without taking account of economic realities, a state which may lead them to discover original, creative, if occasionally impractical design solutions. Subsequently it may be necessary to modify these in order to make them more realistic and workable. But we can sometimes learn a lesson in problem-solving ourselves through the experience of seeing the risk-taking originality of the children we teach.

Happy accidents, like the discovery of stainless steel, or glass tubing (see Osborn, 1948/1972), are apparently few and far between. If the crop of fortunate accidents cannot be increased there must be alternative efforts made deliberately to promote creative thinking. De Bono (1976) suggests that creative thinking can be taught. If that is true, then art and design processes can make a significant contribution. Where else in the curriculum are visual and sometimes irrational fantasies so readily acceptable? Art often gives children the chance to develop impractical ideas as if they already existed. In their representations on paper children regularly enter a world where materials can be given unusual properties. The heaviest of them can temporarily defy gravity, the lightest be given unreasonable toughness. It could well turn out that the irrational, unreasonable and impractical can be an important part of the problem-solving process. If it does, then we may be dealing with a life skill, rather than merely indulging the fantasies of childhood.

Introducing Design and Problem-Solving to Children

It is arguable how old children must be before they can cope with design and problem-solving as activities. Many 5 year-olds may be quite unable to follow a sequence or to predict what they think might happen. Generally their experience of the world and its materials is as yet very limited. The 7 and 8 year-olds may have the capacity to predict what will happen and are much more likely to follow a sequence of anticipated events. That does not mean that young children cannot be introduced to elements of designing, though the approach must be at a much less sophisticated level.

How might this be done? One way is to develop children's drawing as a way of classifying and explaining their ideas about design. When children are old enough to cope with a very simple sequence, one drawing can lead to another to establish the necessary concept of development in a design process. For example, many children's drawings tell a story, almost like a cartoon strip. Drawing 'what might happen next' is an activity closely associated with designing and one which obviously involves prediction as well as sequence. Through drawing out ideas on paper, a child also creates a resource for discussion of how things might work.

There are obviously problems to overcome with the very youngest of children. The essential point to grasp here is that although we may not achieve very much it is important to make a start. Subjects that can be attempted (either as one drawing, as a sequence of drawings, or in verbal and written form) could tackle problems like 'How do you think a bicycle pump works?', 'What happens if we change small wheels for big ones?', or 'How would you design a space craft?'

Besides drawing, basic to designing is an understanding of the nature, properties and qualities of materials. Good designers understand the limitations and potential of the material they choose and through experience gain insight into those qualities and possibilities which each material offers. It follows that worthwhile activities can be set for children so that they can begin to understand more about how different substances behave.

In the first instance this may be as elementary as comparing Plasticine with dough. Later on, children may be finding out the difference between one fabric and another, or comparing the properties of two kinds of adhesive. At the age of 4 or 5 tactile experience is very important and children need to push blocks around, squeeze washing-up liquid bottles, stroke fur and velvet simply to discover the feel of materials. Junk modelling is ideal for finding out about different materials. But the activity needs to be taken seriously if children are to understand that materials are different to handle. Traditionally they may only have used what materials were provided. If we want to develop their discrimination and introduce them to design from the moment they start school, they must begin to talk about these differences in terms of quality and function.

There are many objects of whose function children have no idea. This is especially true of objects from organizations such as the various school museum services. We can ask young children a wide variety of questions like

'Why isn't this made of sand?'

'What might happen if this was made of newspaper?'

'What do you think it would be like if lamp-posts were made of rubber?'

'Why do you think this is made of metal?'

'What do you think your favourite toy is made of?'

'What do you think this object is used for?'

'How would you use this?'

'Can you think of a way to draw this?'

'What else could we use this for?'

Older children might make these comparisons themselves by constructing the same model animal, for instance, from alternatives like sand, Plasticine, clay, Lego, or paper to see how different they are and why. Whilst to a very young child most art materials present practical problems, older children can be introduced to a far wider range to relate them to designing. They can explore materials not only for expressing their artistic ideas but also with a view to designing and making things which could have a purpose. Essentially this is a process of discovery, but seen now with the eye of a designer as well as that of a fine artist.

Materials like adhesives can be compared without specifically posing design problems. In the realms of simple science we may want to test the strength of various glues by hanging weights from the glued objects. Such activities are worthwhile but not necessarily art or design. They can be entirely the province of science and technology. For children to copy the shape of a pebble in clay, however, or to make silhouette shapes in black paper brings them nearer to design considerations. Their concern, in this example, is for form and outline, not solely function. It is also important for them to find out which shapes and materials might conveniently glue together and which will not. There is little point in exploring materials just for the sake of it. They also need to find out what their properties are, how they function, how they are used and how they might be used.

Children can start to develop some awareness of design through looking critically at designed objects in their surroundings. They may not be expected to do this particularly well at first, especially in their early years, but will have made a beginning along the route towards a growing design consciousness. Much later on in their lives we can expect them to have developed some sensitivity to good and bad design. In a good design there ought to be the feeling that no other way of doing things was appropriate. We ought to feel that to change the shape would be to destroy the aesthetic form and make it a poorer design. If the design is bad, we should know why and question what might be done about it.

In the classroom, the cross-curricular implications of introducing design are far-reaching. We can imagine children being set a task like 'Think of three ways of using materials for designing a pattern'. What begins as an elementary design problem may lead to solutions which have an aesthetic and visual content, but will of course offer much more in terms of discussion and learning. The children might make patterns in the sand tray or in clay, which might in turn lead to looking at sand patterns made by the tide on the beach, or patterns found in minerals. Both these natural materials could lead to work which develops in simple science or environmental studies.

Technology also features in many design processes. Children, for example, who are using layers of papier mâché (Chapter 11) are involved in the same process as is used for building up a fibreglass mould. When they model in clay or assemble using collage, they mirror design processes used in advertising. Modelling has been done this way in schools for years so there is nothing very new about it. The new element for teachers is deliberately to make links with these established processes of technology and design and bring them to children's attention. Design consciousness must inevitably take account of the technology which it encompasses.

In the more traditional way we have taught children art, problem-solving is generally of two kinds. Children face practical problems, like how to glue and fasten things together, how to mix paints, or how to control a medium like clay. And there are imaginative ideas-related problems. Like how to draw a machine designed to perform a variety of household tasks, or how to design a painting of 'Seven Swans a-Swimming'. Specific design problems emerge each time any project has a set of imposed limitations or functions (like seven swans rather than six or eight, or a device for household tasks rather than for brain surgery). In fine art there is a certain freedom and autonomy. In design there is often the imposition of limitations and functions. Fine artists need be accountable only to themselves, but designers are usually bound by a design brief. Where the limitations of that design brief are very clearly stated, the solutions often present a considerable challenge.

Of course, art and design overlap and are not mutually exclusive. This very feature blurs the edges between art and design and makes defining design extremely difficult. Whilst it may be true that function plays a much stronger role in design than it does in art, we can still see examples of the process working within traditional art activities. Children already engage in designing. It could even be said that design is the structure of any art form. Without design it lacks order, coherence and successful organization of the elements of line, colour, shape, tone and texture. These elements defy any rules we care to invent for designing because each artistic structure is different and therefore unique.

An example of the way these limitations are imposed on fine art is seen at Christmas time. There are already a number of expectations (e.g. Father Christmas will be red and angels need wings). Originality and problem-solving are severely put to the test, especially in an area where artwork has gathered a tradition of festive stereotypes. Yet precisely because there are limitations to the colours, forms and functions of

Christmas artefacts, children respond as designers, answerable to a design brief. This may sound impressive and of exaggerated status, but children are designing and have been doing so in schools for many years.

We associate problem-solving with design perhaps more than we do with art. Yet problem-solving is not confined to design alone. Many problems in the traditional 'fine art' area of drawing and painting are well known and arise with some frequency. In fine art there are visual problems for children to solve like

(1) how to arrange the subject on the paper
(2) representing imagined three-dimensional space
(3) making one shape or colour stand out against another
(4) choosing the most appropriate medium
(5) deciding on size and scale
(6) finding shape and content which best expresses the ideas
(7) organizing and handling painting materials
(8) trying to make the colour green from primaries red, yellow and blue.

The older they get, the more sophisticated seem the problems children set themselves. As children move from symbols to visual realism (Chapter 4) they face considerable difficulty in dealing with the illusion of space. Very young children are often far less worried about where to place things on their paper, whereas 6, 7 and 8 year-olds become much more concerned with problems of how to represent space. Drawing problems are not new, yet they still need to be solved. A designer is not after all like a machine which switches off and on, depending on whether it is dealing with art or design. There is some support for the view that design has its roots in 'fine art' rather than technology (as has been promoted in two well-constructed programmes, 'Design Matters', BBC Television, September 1985).

Stages in Problem-Solving

When we turn to design ideas, it can be argued that problem-solving takes on similar characteristics to problems of designing in the 'fine art' tradition. Function, fitness for purpose, or economic practicality are of course factors, but for the designer aesthetic considerations are also of equal and occasionally greater importance. A motor vehicle, for example, must not only function. We expect that if it is to sell to the public it will also be a pleasing shape. In a design process there is a design logic to take into account. Sometimes the logical process is that there are stages where facts are gathered, needs identified, ideas and solutions generated and finally put to the test. By contrast, in the world of industrial design, facts may be thin on the ground, needs difficult to identify and many mistakes made. Although we may think it is useful to teach children a reassuring and consistently logical process of design, it is precisely this logic which can limit outcomes. As David Pye (1978) has pointed out,

> It is eminently true of design that if you are not prepared to make mistakes you will never make anything at all.

Such approaches as there are must take account of a wide variety of factors and try out unlikely processes and solutions, If we are to introduce children to problem-solving as an art activity in its own right we need to be wary of a commonly experienced pitfall. Whenever we are faced with a problem to solve, a temptation is to expect that there is one problem and therefore ultimately one workable solution. In fact there are usually several problems and several possible solutions. Part of the skill of problem-solving lies in developing the ability to identify these several problems, generate many solutions to them and choose from the best.

Five important stages in design and problem-solving are evident and offer a flexible model. Most other models produced by design educators tend to be variations of this one, but its roots are in common sense rather than conceptual theory. The first stage is to examine and collect information about the problem. This is the point at which it is quite likely we will discover that the problem is (as already discussed) several problems. We can call this early stage 'Information Gathering'. Suppose we asked a group of children to design a 'spacesuit' for a school play. They might consider a variety of questions like

'What would we need to think about if we had a particular person in mind?'
'What characteristics does it need if it is to fit most people?'
'Should it have any special working parts?'
'What materials would work best?'
'Should we just design it or do we need to make it as well to find out if it works, fits and looks good?'

Stage two would be to allow imagination to run riot and generate both practical and impractical ideas. This we can refer to as 'Idea Generation'. A spacesuit made of metal would obviously be heavy and impractical, but to consider making it of metal might be the very thought which later proves useful. To disregard the impractical at this stage would be unfortunate. For example, the suit might, finally, include metal foil and bottle tops in its construction. By discussing metal as a material we might eventually find ourselves talking about the design of suits of armour. There are many designs for armour which are both functional and artistic, and comparisons of both aspects of design can prove useful teaching points (even if we began by designing a spacesuit). What, for instance, does a suit of armour need as a design feature compared with the requirements of a spacesuit?

In an earlier chapter (Chapter 5) mention was made of the 'Scamper' technique of idea generation. In essence there is no difference between trying to think of ideas for teaching and trying to generate ideas as solutions to problems. Once we have thought of only a few ideas, the processes of rearranging, altering, substituting, eliminating and so on, are useful tools of design development. Unless, however, they are consciously applied (as in the Scamper technique), important alternatives can go ignored. Every possible means should be used to generate new lines of thinking and no strategy for doing this may be ruled out.

If we really want to generate ideas it is worth deliberately setting out to stimulate thinking by imposing odd limitations and trying oblique avenues of enquiry. The process is one which seems to send messages to what we could call the brain's 'Creative Department'. It may be that nothing needs to be adapted, added to, or rearranged. On the other hand, by consciously sitting down to make ourselves think of alternatives, adaptations, substitutions and rearrangements, we stand a far better chance of stumbling on something new.

Stage three is to construct the design, which may be a very crude prototype, something we can look at before proceeding further. During the making we will inevitably touch on other stages in the process, but for convenience only, we can describe this stage as 'Making'. From making we can move to 'Evaluating'. Stage four is to test and evaluate the design solutions in order to change and finally choose the most promising of them. Naturally, the younger the children are, the less they can be expected to devise ideas which are brilliantly practical. They are therefore not going to respond well to an over-critical appraisal of their creative but impractical solutions. When we are in the judgemental realms of good, bad, better and best, the competitive element can easily become destructive of children's confidence. Yet they can be involved in simple checking and testing, which is a valuable experience for later more sophisticated problem-solving and evaluating.

In doing this, there is an obvious comparison for them to make their initial identification of the problem. How has it been solved? What problems emerged as work progressed? What changes were made to the original design and what difference did they make? Individual children can compare and discuss their own solutions, one with another, to see what they themselves think are the best features. Very little is to be gained at this age from urging children to pick out and criticize the worst elements of a design solution. If the aim is to find out what works, then children need to understand at the outset that condemning the solutions for their impracticality does not usually move them far forward (a view which flies in the face of much human experience but is true of very many instances of problem-solving). To ask how the best of their solutions might be improved can be far more constructive.

In the evaluating part of the process we should ask not only what looks best but why one idea is better than another. Children are not naturally inclined to analyse why one feature of a design is better. Neither in many instances are adults, and to be able to pinpoint what advantages one solution has over another is a sophisticated skill which needs practice and experience to develop it. We can at least make a start, however, by asking simple questions which are likely to promote evaluation. In group discussions we can ask,

'Why do you think this would work?'

'Why do you think this part is the best?'

'What do you think of its appearance?'

'How could you improve it?'

'What does this do?'

'How might it be made to work better?'

'If you had to change this what would you do?'

'If you had to add something what would it be?'

To 'Modify' the design is a very obvious step before finally adopting the best solution. Again there are shades of the Scamper technique mentioned earlier, though if we are to achieve total flexibility in handling design, perhaps we should not think of all these stages in this order alone. They usually react and interact with each other. We therefore have to think of five stages which in differing circumstances will demand different patterns of usage. The whole sequence (1) to (5) might occur over and over again, or a stage might need to be left out, another one added. For convenience the stages are

(1) information gathering
(2) idea generation
(3) making
(4) evaluating
(5) modifying.

Many good design solutions quickly attract the support and attention of simple science to make them work. It is not difficult to imagine a child's design for a multi-purpose machine soon needing to take account of things like motors and wheels. Our concern here though is with art. The aesthetic must never become an afterthought but permeate the design process as it evolves. Considerations of shape, colour, line, texture and tone are still the designer's tools for production and there is no reason why they should not be considered at the earliest stage of designing. Sensitivity to aesthetic qualities which exist in good design is not learned by rote. Children will learn far more about design by designing things themselves and looking at everything with the critical eye of a designer. Inevitably, to develop any sensitivity to design is to encourage children to look at what surrounds them, not only the man-made 'designed' objects, but natural forms as well. A major area of study and discussion is the form and aesthetic characteristics of things which are in nature and have influence on the designer. These are the resources for shape, proportion and function. Nature offers the designer a great variety of examples from which to learn.

Nowhere is this more evident than in the superb designs to be found in sea shells, rocks, minerals, animals and plants, all of which demonstrate principles of design. We need only look at how leaf stems grow out of the main body of a plant to see how structurally sound they are. Thicker stems bear heavier weight and the whole plant grows according to its function and surrounding conditions. The Passiflora (Passion Flower, Figure 31) is a good example of design in a plant whose tendrils have a specific function, working rather like small springs as it clings to its surroundings. Beyond function, its flower head is considered a master-piece of artistic design. From nature we derive many of our most aesthetically pleasing curves, harmonies and contrasts. They are not

Figure 31 Passiflora.

difficult to find, nor can we find a much better starting place for awakening children's sensitivity to them.

Practical Examples

All the design projects which follow can have practical outcomes. However, the discussion and comparisons children make as they evaluate and change designs are just as important as the final product. In some instances the teacher may feel that discussion is far more important than drawing and designing. It may be that the only design-related activity is discussing an aspect of these examples. It would be unreasonable to suppose these projects could stay entirely in the domain of art and design. They may suggest all areas of the curriculum despite the fact that here they emphasize the aesthetic, artistic and visual side of design.

These ideas can be developed to encompass discussion of both contemporary and historical material. Here, and in the brief examples which follow, there is no indication of the learning concepts and problem-solving involved. This is quite deliberate. No activity is worthwhile without being a relevant part of the curriculum, but it is the task of the teacher to make purposeful links with children's growing experience, rather than begin a design activity which does not fit in with ongoing work. For the format to be educationally worthwhile, these ideas would certainly need to take account of many of the categories of learning already discussed in previous chapters (see especially the format in Chapter 8).

SHOPS AND HOUSES

Children's existing classroom surroundings are an obvious starting point for devising design activities. A Home Corner (Wendy House), for instance, can become a source of design. Whenever children organize space and furniture, they are designing, even though the level of this activity does not appear to be very sophisticated. They can usefully consider the design of their play space according to its function, layout and appearance. Questions might be,

'If you could change this room what would you do?'

'How does the builder design houses so that the rain doesn't run down the walls?'

'How do windows open?'

'How do you think the rooms in a house are used?'

'What is it like in the Wizard's Lair?' (story, drama)

They can also organize a classroom shop, a well-tried activity which is rich in potential for designing not just the one shop but extending to include

shop fronts, consideration of lettering, decoration and displays

food, sweets, sweet wrappers, chocolate boxes, sweet containers

packaging, posters, advertisements

shop interiors, counters, check-outs, tills

sale goods: clothing, hardware, bicycles, vegetables, groceries, electrical goods, televisions and radios, computers

gardening supplies, decorators

butchers, bakers, antiques.

Design ideas should also lead to other related ideas. For example, shop tills have changed dramatically from the hand-operated to the electronic, computer-based pay points of today. Comparison of their designs can lead to a study of shape in relation to materials, decoration and clothing fashions. Similarly, designing patterns for clothing may develop in the direction of looking at designs for hats, boots, shoes, dresses and skirts. Obviously, hats can be designed for specific jobs, like helmets for firemen, welders or astronauts. Alternatively, they can become more imaginative like 'My Automatic Hat', or 'Party Hats', which may prompt yet another design theme.

DESIGN FOR A PARTY (OLDER CHILDREN)

The children are asked to design on paper and write about a place outside or inside where they would hold a party. The emphasis could be on the information-gathering stage of design. They must next choose their colours and dream up shapes and surroundings which they would like to find there. They should consider themselves to be like stage designers who have been given unlimited funds to design an environment. They have to think of what specially designed costumes they might wear and who or what else would come to the Party. This could include imaginary creatures, changing scenery, lights and sound, and creating events or technical devices for entertainment. The whole theme could produce several different areas of design and discussion. An important aspect of this project would be to discuss what design problems there might be and how they could be overcome.

ADVENTURES

Problem-solving activities can grow from reading stories with children. The stories which have an adventure theme are particularly useful. They can provide inspiration for drawing and painting, or children may construct using modelling materials.

'Draw (tell me, write) how you would escape from the cave.'
'What would you need to cross the river?'
'How do you think you would use these?'
'How would you climb over the rocks?'
'How can you cross this crevasse?'
'How would you get past the fiery dragon?'
'What obstacles could you invent if it was your story?'

'How would you find the treasure?' (Links with simple map work. Draw a map of how you come to school, a treasure map, or a map of school buildings.)

From the questions above, children might make models of their imagined solutions in paper, clay, or Plasticine. Or the solutions could provide them with subject matter for drawings and paintings. The projects could be extended into simple science or mathematical activities, but to keep the art and design perspective, considerations of the shapes, colours, arrangement and function would still be essential.

JEWELLERY

Geometric and mathematical designs can inspire some children to design jewellery. The process of enamelling is beyond many young children, but they can still produce large drawings of jewelled adornments. There is also a vast resource of illustrations available for the study of things like bangles, rings, brooches and pendants down the ages. Children love designing things which involve decoration and pattern, especially if they can be worn. If the scale of the designs is enlarged to make drawing and colouring much easier they become effective as displays for study and discussion. Only some of them need to be made to scale. A professional designer very often works on a scale much larger than the final product. Additionally, it may be possible to design using collage materials, strong glue and a glue gun (finally producing something to wear in drama, the 'Shop' or the 'Home Corner').

DESIGN SOME SWEETS

This can be treated as a study of pattern, or as a design for an imaginative confection. Children might design a special patterned sweet, such as 'Liquorice Allsorts', or create an imaginary sweet shop full of their own designs. They could collect and compare the design of packaging and sweet wrappers.

VARIATIONS ON THE SWEETS

Birthday cakes, feasts, fantasies such as sugar houses, sugar mountains and foods of all kinds provide stimuli for design. The best chefs are involved in design as they create their special dishes. Children could imagine they are 'Best Chefs' and design as if they considered that the visual presentation of their food could be as interesting as its taste.

TEXTILE DESIGN

Simple prints, such as those discussed in Chapter 10, can be a good starting point for looking at printed textiles. Children can begin to design their own through looking at costume, furnishing fabrics like curtains, tapestries and wall hangings. Once children have developed the skill of following their own pencil line with a printing block, they can manage more complex patterns. Fabric designs can evolve from simple ruler-drawn patterns. Some may repeat, others be much more random.

DESIGNS FOR FLOORING

This has links with mathematics through tessellation and symmetry. The children begin by making a collage from small squares of paper. Different colours can be used, paint manufacturers' shade cards, anything which will produce a regular tile pattern. A mathematical link can be made with Logi-blocs, rectangles, triangles, squares and hexagons. It may be possible to obtain flooring samples where children can see how designs fit together. They might draw on paper and fill in with pencil, felt-tip, or pen, arranging tiles using a number sequence. This could be done by numbering the squares, for example, 1, 3, 4, 7, 11, 7, 4, 3, 1 (counting on from the last square which was numbered), and choosing a numbered colour to fill in the design, continuing all the way down a whole page of squares. Variations and extensions of this idea are numerous and can readily be discussed alongside work in number. Children could alternatively make designs based on the maths work they are doing.

A further development would be to design floor mosaics so that although smaller paper shapes might be used, the idea would be to produce a regular floor mosaic with a decorative border. Reference to Roman mosaics, shopping arcades and murals would be a valuable starting point, though often children respond far better to historical mosaics after they have tried to design one themselves. There are also a number of tiled mosaics in the London Underground.

MURALS

Not all murals are neatly rectangular and many street murals are painted on gable ends and in odd shapes. Children can design murals to fit a cut-out shape of a gable, possibly an end-of-terrace house. Young children would need to see examples of the shape and might benefit from seeing photographs of murals other artists have done. They could also try to design a mural for a specific building, like a railway station, a school, a hospital, or a library. Reference for murals is much more common than it used to be, especially in London and other major cities of Britain where there are a number of gable-end murals.

AEROPLANES AND DREAM CARS

When we think of design, man-made objects feature as important examples. Many children will eagerly see themselves as the designers of racing cars, custom-built cars, aircraft and spaceships. There are plenty of examples of children, especially boys, designing these vehicles time after time in their art sessions. In design education there can be a much more serious enquiry into function as well as fantasy. What would their ideal dream car do that other cars do not? How might an aircraft function if it could do other things besides fly? What else could we make it do that would be useful?

MACHINES

A variation on the idea of designing vehicles is to think about designing fantastic machines. Instead of this being limited to designing a machine to solve problems we already know about, the project can be reversed. The brief is 'Design a machine which has wheels, levers and buttons. Now think of about six things your machine might be for. What do you think it does now you have designed it?' Variations could be devised to include robots, mechanical arms and imaginary machine-like creatures. Specific ideas might be 'The Best-Ever Food Machine', 'The Greatest Cleaner in the World', or 'The Get-You-Up-In-The-Morning Machine'.

DIRT EATER

Here the children are involved in social, economic and technical issues as well as design. Their task is to design a machine (or think of a fantasy creature) which eats the rubbish left by humans. Designs can be three-dimensional, or drawings, or may for much of the time be something written down and discussed.

MIND STRETCHERS

These are design problems intended to stretch the imagination. Some of them are impossible situations requiring an acceptance of fantasy as well as development of creative thinking. (Judgement is needed to assess the appropriate age-range for these tasks.)

(1)   Design a fish which you think could live in transparent school glue. Show how it would swim.

(2)   Imagine we never needed to sleep. Draw a design for a house where there are no bedrooms and think of new uses for the rooms.

(3)   Design a bottle that has outlets at the top, bottom and sides. How would you use it?

(4)   Imagine that in the school corridor there are ten levers and five buttons. Draw a design showing what you think the levers and buttons might do.

Finally, it must be said that one effect of being involved in design education is that the teacher can participate in thinking about how to solve problems. An essential ingredient in a teacher's preparation is to think of questions like

'What might we need to think about if we designed a mural?'

'What do we need to think about if we design a racing car?'

'What do we need to consider to design a fabric?'

Although questions like these can motivate us to think in new ways ourselves, the temptation to supply answers for the children needs to be resisted. Design education in the early years of schooling is so new it is destined to change the way in which we have previously thought about teaching art. Yet it need not conflict with any vision of artistic growth we privately hold. The responsibility for developing children artistically at school is ultimately ours. How much design education we include depends partly on our own interests and preferences, partly on the way we see it developing in the next decade. It is a facet of art which enhances and enriches our existing heritage. We always need to consider carefully what anything new will displace, and should be aware of the importance of design in relation to fine art, not as a subject divorced from any part of the art curriculum.

159

13

Assessment and Evaluation

FEW AREAS lend themselves so readily to the unquestioned criticism of being subjective as do the assessment and evaluation of art. Some teachers would say that nothing worthwhile can be assessed or evaluated in art and anyone who tries is fooling themselves if they think it can. The argument grows from the stance that however carefully we judge anything artistic, because that judgement is personal and therefore subjective, it is not valid in comparison with other judgements. Of course, if our starting point has been that art itself has no value, is a frill, a recreation, or a time-filler, there is little to be argued. The basis of informed judgement is that we should know something of the values which permeate the area of our concern.

Assessment of major works of art by painters such as Van Gogh or Rembrandt would prove just as difficult a task as the assessment of children's work. The criteria for assessing can lead to a nonsense. Could we say that Van Gogh's handling of colour was masterly where Rembrandt's was not? Could we say that Rembrandt achieved a higher standard of drawing? Would we say, as we handled a tear-stained piece of paper, that because a famous poet cried bitterly whilst writing the lines, the poem must be deeply emotional? Each artist's work is valued for qualities over and above the mundane. To assess in a naive or mechanistic way is to ignore what brings fame to the artist.

We are not dealing with the famous, but suppose we were teaching children art in the United States of America. It is more than likely we would pay as much attention to the development of their personalities through art as we would to the artwork they produced. We might even see the development of a child's personality as the main reason for teaching. In some other countries and cultures art education clearly has a different emphasis. There are also questions of how reliable or credible assessments and evaluations are, what their function is and how we should arrive at judgements. To complicate matters further it is not always clear what can be evaluated and what may not.

Who is to assess and evaluate? What seems excellent to one teacher may not be seen the same way by other teachers, HMI, parents, or children. A piece of work, or progress in maturing personality, may be exceptional compared with previous examples from an individual child. But how are we to know?

For the purposes of this chapter, evaluation is perceived as a process through which we determine the value of what we are doing or have done. This is usually understood to be the educational value, though by that broad term we could also mean learning about oneself in relation to the arts, or ultimately to life itself. Evaluation tends to take place over a period of time or is encountered periodically at an appropriate point in a course of learning. It is often characterized by reflection on the extent to which our aims and objectives have been achieved. Evaluation particularly focuses upon our own teaching though of course we can also evaluate children's progress in terms of achievement.

Assessment, in this instance, is taken to mean making judgements using known criteria to determine whether particular qualities or changes are evident and skills or abilities have been acquired. There are many forms of assessment and many terms which can be used to describe them, ranging from ongoing informal assessment to formal procedures involving detailed testing and grading (see Rowntree, 1977). Yet if the process is not to become unwieldy (since the aim is to produce a useful account of a child's artistic development), the definition and method of assessment must be accessible and readily understood. Assessment in the model proposed here seeks to identify qualities and skills by means of an assessment schedule, a format based on assessment profiles.

All assessment procedures have limitations, even those associated with measurement. In fact for some teachers assessment is solely associated with measurement, though as David Best (1983) has commented,

It is crucial to recognize that only some kinds of progress can be measured.

Moreover, the most important aspects of educational progress, such as the ability to understand people, and moral and emotional development, cannot be measured, although they certainly can be assessed.

Assessment is concerned, for our purposes, with trying to discover what the child has achieved or become. Evaluation enables the teacher to reflect upon a session, programme of work, or period of teaching. Through evaluation an attempt is made to identify the effects and effectiveness of teaching, and assessment is a necessary part of this. We may, for example, assess a child's progress in relation to his previous work or in some instances that of his particular class or group.

To assess or evaluate anything in the arts we need first to be aware of the context in which the art is produced or the process takes place. The time, location, values and attitudes all have a bearing on how we form judgements. This view is shared by a number of art educators and is a corner-stone of the Assessment of Performance Unit (DES APU Aesthetic Development, 1983) and of work by Eisner (1972). There would be little point in judging a 4 year-old's painting against that of a teenager, sculpture against painting, or colour against black and white.

Nor should we become victim of arguments which suggest art cannot be assessed because it is too subjective. David Best declares the opposite by arguing that assessment of art is objective. But we need to revise common assumptions about what it is to be objective, not only in the arts, but in the sciences. He points out that judgements in science are, despite the empirical research which they encompass, given their sense by underlying theoretical interpretation. That is, interpretation is just as important in the sciences as it is in the arts. As Best states, not all objective assessments are scientific, and scientific examination cannot tell us all that can be objectively known about human behaviour. It certainly cannot tell us what is most important in human life.

It is not that the arts are like the sciences in yielding definitive conclusions, but, on the contrary, that the sciences are like the arts in their ultimate answerability to new and different interpretation of objective features.

(Best, 1985)

The arguments Best puts forward are not just academic quibbles. We should not be misled by the fact that testing and measuring are frequently not only associated with assessment but erroneously equated with it. Testing and measuring sometimes have irresistible attractions in that written proof can be pointed to and data produced as clear evidence of progress. Yet the measurable, quantifiable aspects of education are not very helpful when it comes to assessing whether or not certain qualities are evident, qualities such as expression, feeling, imagination, or invention. That they cannot be quantified, or scientifically verified, certainly does not mean that they cannot be assessed, for instance, by a sensitive teacher's judgement.

The range of professional interpretations of progress in artistic development can be wide but it is by no means unlimited. There is also some consensus amongst experienced teachers about what constitutes poor or exceptional progress. Even so, an understanding of children's capabilities and their expected development is clearly something we would need for assessing any progress children make, whether in mathematics, language, or art. Where judgement does not include testing and measuring we may simply need more tolerance of differing interpretations. Even if we are faced with a set of figures or test results, the process of assessing anything still calls for experience and professional interpretation. Test results are not always conclusive proof of existing ability.

For this reason it is essential to develop educational and artistic values which can be articulated and defended. If we are to recognize specific qualities in children's work or personal progress we must first have experience of what those qualities are. There would be little point, for example, determining whether or not a child was capable of mixing colours from a strong red to a paler shade of pink, unless we knew what these shades looked like. We would similarly need to have experience of what might be expected from children at a certain age to judge how far a child had developed artistically for his age.

An Assessment Model

The model offered in Chart 6 comprises five categories and a variety of criteria for forming judgements. Typically a scale of one to five could be used to assign a grade but this can encourage a great number of grade three marks. For this example a scale of one to six is used though one to ten could be substituted. It should also be pointed out that alternative improvements to these criteria can be added or substituted for those printed here. Given that we must be aware of the context in which children work, the following categories are chosen for convenience only.

(1) *Process of Working* This covers the important aspects of artistic development during the action of creating artwork. Certain abilities like developing an idea, changing the design, substituting, adding and improving are not otherwise evident except during the process of working. Response to ideas and visual stimuli are sometimes far more evident during the process than they are in the final product.

(2) *Handling of Materials* It is important to know whether or not children have developed good organizational skills and can use a variety of materials appropriately. This is quite without regard to the artistic outcomes. We need, for instance, to know if children can organize and use paints as a prerequisite to producing a worthwhile painting, or scissors if they are cutting out a shape. Otherwise there is a considerable gap between intention and skill needed to handle materials.

(3) *Use of Media* Apart from the control of materials we need to know whether or not children are developing an understanding of the media they use. Can they, for example, mix colours together to produce shades? Do they simply draw with paint or can they use it in other ways (e.g. to produce textures, patterns, blocks of colour)? Can they design models in clay which make the best use of the medium?

(4) *Critical Skills* This category deals with discriminatory skills and is concerned with looking and analysing. Children do not only produce artwork, they develop the ability to discriminate between one colour and another, different lines and different shapes. They can be involved from an early age with looking at designs and artwork by other artists as well as at their own work. They will also need to look at their natural environment in a critical way, comparing such varied designs and patterns as those on leaves or sea shells. Critical skills can also include self-assessment for which older children (7–9 years) might use a self-assessment sheet.

(5) *Stages of Personal Development* This covers assessment in relation to the expected stages for the age-range. As Eisner (1972) says, these stages are simply an indication of what children might be expected to do when left to their own devices. In order to make judgements we need to refer to stages of developing imagery (as outlined in Chapter 4) but bear in mind that the aim is not to rush children through these stages. The aim is to see how far they have developed as a result of engaging in artwork. Besides this, there are social and personal attitudes to art such as the degree to which children value their own and other children's work. To

what extent, for example, are they able to accept praise and criticism of their own work?

Chart 6 An Assessment Model

NAME: AGE: 7 yrs 8 mths   CLASS: 3   DATE:

	MARK/YEAR						COMMENTS
(1) *Process of Working*	1	2	3	4	5	6	
Is inventive, full of ideas							
Shows initiative, independence							
Shows curiosity and interest when working							
Puts in effort							
Perseveres with artwork							
Is keen, absorbed when working							
Works well with others							
Responds to visual stimuli, ideas							
Able to overcome difficulties							
Can follow instructions when necessary							
(2) *Handling of Materials*							
Able to mix paint to good consistency							
Can use a variety of drawing media							
Able to use scissors							
Understands nature of media, e.g. Plasticine Clay							

	MARK/YEAR						COMMENTS
	1	2	3	4	5	6	
(3) *Use of Media*							
Discriminates when choosing colours							
Shows skill in mixing colours							
Able to use a paintbrush appropriately to the medium							
Able to use modelling/3-D media							
Can select appropriate media where choice is offered							
(4) *Critical Skills*							
Responds enthusiastically to looking at artwork							
Able to discuss ideas and experiences							
Can point out similarities and differences in things seen							
Keenly observant of environment							
Notices displays, things brought in							
Able to use artistic vocabulary, e.g. colour, line, shape, dark, light							
Able to make judgements about own performance or achievement							
(5) *Stages of Personal Development*							
Work is at appropriate stage of development for age of child							

	MARK/YEAR						COMMENTS
	1	2	3	4	5	6	
Sees links with other areas of learning, e.g. mathematics							
Has confidence in producing artwork							
Able to tackle subjects involving the emotions							
Adapts to changes of ideas							
Values own work							
Values the work of others							
Helps others							
Able to accept criticism							
Able to cope with praise							
Listens attentively							
Is able to say why s/he likes or dislikes aspects of artwork							

Evaluation

As teachers we are sometimes our own worst enemy when evaluating. Self-criticism is frequently interpreted as merely finding fault with our own teaching, a practice which could lead to frustration and a poor sense of personal worth. This is not true of all teachers but is far more commonly found than it need be. None of us really believes that we teach perfectly or that nothing can ever be improved. Although the very word evaluate suggests that we determine the value of something, in practice we can often misinterpret this as looking for what is not of value, rather than what is.

These two aspects of evaluation are admittedly like sides of the same coin but need not become unbalanced and tend to the negative. If evaluation is to be useful (and this usually means it leads to changes in the way we or the children work) it should be seen as a signpost for the future rather than a condemnation of the past. The future cannot be evaluated, but there is something to be said for evaluating past performance with an eye to making changes. Where evaluation is solely a judgement on the past, it can quickly become fixed and impotent, a fair account of the past but no indicator of future developments.

Teachers evaluate most of the time. It is hardly possible to think about what children might do next without evaluating what has gone before. They may need more practice in colour-mixing, for instance, or a drawing might reveal skills which could be used in another context. It could be that particular developing skills in using pattern should be put to a different use. By this (often subconscious) means of evaluation, artistic learning can be given direction rather than remaining random or without impetus.

There are evaluation questions which refer to several aspects of art teaching. In a previous chapter (Chapter 7) evaluation was inevitably introduced when the topics listed for discussion of children's artwork were introduced. It would be very difficult not to discuss artwork without simultaneously evaluating something in connection with the work. Mention has also been made (Chapter 12) of the evaluation process as a stage in the proposed model for designing. Other than this, there are questions we can ask ourselves, like

How well are the children motivated?

Was the stimulus appropriate?

Does the organization work well? (e.g. water pots, paints)

How original is the thinking? (e.g. compared with copying other children's/teacher's ideas)

Was good use made of things brought in from home?

How well is the drawing developing?

Can the children use reference material like pictures and photographs without copying?

How inventive is the work?

How well is the chosen medium used?

How extensively is this theme/project developed?

How well can the children mix colours which are light in tone as well as dark?

How varied is the range of materials the children can use?

How well do they tackle subjects concerned with emotion?

Have they any particular flair for using pattern?

How imaginative are the pieces of work?

Are the children able to take care in colouring a shape they have drawn or cut out?

Record-Keeping

An attractive criterion for record-keeping is that its administration should not be cumbersome. Alongside the rest of the school records it need not be complicated to write up or difficult to understand. Evaluating, assessing and record-keeping can be tedious if they are not streamlined processes. If they are especially over-elaborate they also run the risk of being confusing rather than clearly illuminating the general picture of pupil progress.

A simple form of record-keeping would be to have the assessment schedule indicated above (or a version of it) and have two pieces of the child's work. Space in school is at a premium so that more than two pieces is generous. A suggestion is that one of these pieces should be a drawing. Drawings are revealing of the child's stage of development especially if they include people (see Chapter 4). The work which is eventually kept for reference should ideally be a good example of that child's ability, clearly labelled and dated. This is not always possible but it can be argued that to have some work kept back is better than none at all.

Comments which are written on the assessment schedule are usually far more revealing of the child's development than are grades. A narrative style like 'Rebecca has produced some interesting paintings of animals and can use colour well. She needs to be more tidy and careful when using a brush' conveys in a sentence or two some of the aspects of her work. Although the narrative approach is not very detailed, its purpose is to point out the main features of progress rather than cover the whole range of areas which might be commented on.

Finally, when records are passed on to another member of staff, or another school (or parents if it is a school report), they should have agreed meanings. Sometimes this is made clear through meetings of parents and teachers. Alternatively it may be necessary to preface the record by describing the way in which the assessment has been made. Without agreed meanings or explanations a variety of misunderstandings can occur. No two teachers assess exactly the same way and each interprets assessments slightly differently from the other. Assessment and evaluation can never be entirely reliable processes. Yet there is no reason why they should not be valuable. Their success will depend on our making the best possible judgements we can at the time. We are dealing with assessments of quality, for which there are no absolute yardsticks. There are sound judgements which, it cannot be emphasized too strongly, call for considerable sensitivity to the qualities of art and design.

14

Conclusions

A FEW years ago, BBC Television ran a series in which portrait painters and sculptors demonstrated their art. One artist was working on a bust of Lord Lichfield, the well-known photographer, and made hundreds of measurements of his face using callipers. These she transferred to a life-size bust made in clay. When she was quite sure that measurements like the length of the nose, chin, mouth and forehead were absolutely accurate, she stopped for a moment. 'You see?' she said. 'It doesn't look right, does it?' She then proceeded to put clay where flesh did not exist and to make lines and twists of expression within the face. Gradually the bust seemed to bear a closer relation to its sitter, rather as if artistic expression had nothing to do with all these preliminary measurements. The artist had to find her own way.

In much the same spirit, good art teaching depends on being a creative teacher who does more than make measurements and look for textbook ways of doing things. Once we have grasped some of the essential characteristics of teaching art, we can leave them behind and find our own ways. It is not nearly so important to read about the value of art as it is to discover for ourselves what artistic values we hold. There is similarly little point in using ideas from preceding chapters without trying to adapt them to suit the artistic learning we have in mind. Ideas and examples often provide the stimuli for developing our own personal artistic ideology (something we ought genuinely to believe in) rather than a repertoire of activities which have no relationship one with another.

A crucial aim of this book has been to present material in such a way that it provokes thought and demands judgement. No book can ever do justice to the variety of teaching styles which affect how we use ideas. Even so, we can examine almost any idea and extend it ourselves by thinking of slight variations. If we suspect that is impossible, more than likely the children we teach will show us how. The essence of good art teaching is to harness the creative ability which is already part of every child. We are catalyst, enquirer, developer and delegator to the creative young minds we try to teach.

Of course, we may begin by organizing activities in a sequenced and directed way, where we always provide the stimulus and present options from which children choose. But as our experience develops, more and more of what children themselves offer can become our stimulus for teaching art. Those teachers who say that everything comes from the children themselves are quite right, although what they say is not always very helpful to the rest of us. Our children are ultimately the creators of any original work which is produced in the classroom and it is they who must learn to look closely, use their imagination, and express their surroundings through art. That is, provided we allow them the opportunity to do so.

The clichés of art teaching may always be with us. It would be foolish to suggest otherwise. Art at Christmas time, decorated paper plates and art for Mother's Day are activities which are best seen for what they are. They are of important social value and will not go away as readily as some art educators would wish them to. Yet they need only take up a fraction of the year's art programme and should not be taken too seriously as constituting artistic learning. As has been pointed out earlier (Chapter 3), they can be adapted to become creative and educationally sound.

A principle which underlies many of the ideas put forward is that of self-responsibility. Each chapter has been written with the intention of providing for, and even encouraging, the exercise of personal choice. When children or teachers are involved in the process of making choices, they are inevitably manipulating thoughts and ideas. This is as true for the child who chooses a range of colours as it is for the teacher who decides why a particular artistic theme will be worth exploring.

In the most creative of classrooms we will often find children deeply absorbed in solving problems for themselves. Their teachers act as guides and illuminators of yet more areas of enquiry and curiosity. The occurrence of this is by no means as rare as might be thought. Most of us have our best and worst moments in teaching and some of the best learning seems to take place when the outcome is a little uncertain. Teacher and children work together to find out what they can about what they can see and feel. It takes little imagination to realize that one of the rewards of teaching art is to become just as interested in what children discover as they are.

An obvious and fundamental teaching skill has already been mentioned: that of drawing children's attention to the appearance of things around them. For some children, their teacher may be the first person to do this with any serious intention of initiating artistic learning. The effect of this apparently simple activity can be very profound and in many instances have a long-lasting influence. It is, however, a skill which needs to be handled with considerable care and insight. Within the apparently simple process of leading children to give attention to looking at things, there is a wealth of subtlety to be discovered.

This is not a plea to put the visual appearance of things above every other educational consideration. It is just as important to count, measure and describe in words as it is to discover through art. The claim made here is that the means of developing artistic awareness are often far less easily understood than more conventional forms of knowledge. In view of this, teaching children to be visually aware may need greater deliberate attention than we give it in our schools today. Although children's artistic development requires the same attention to detail that other subject areas enjoy, in practice it frequently seems to have less than its fair share of the teacher's time.

Through art we have the opportunity to give a significant start to children's early education. The arts, as the Gulbenkian Report (1982) points out, are not only for communicating ideas, *they are ways of having ideas*. As such they can often be the main source of inspiration for the remaining areas of the school curriculum. Through art, children can retain that sense of wonder and delight which all too easily becomes lost as later concerns of adult life take over. Where being an adult can mean there are a variety of unavoidable routine commitments, art, as Elliot Eisner (1972) says, can vitalize life by drawing attention to the quality of experience as such. He comments,

> Art reminds us that the act of looking intensely, of opening one's sensibilities to the environment yields a qualitative reward in the process of living.

This relationship of art and life can be taken still further. If in later life we take up one job in preference to another, we may develop special skills but are bound to neglect others. Consequently we rule out a variety of experiences which there is no time for us to enjoy. The quality of our jobs and interests can determine the quality of our lives just as easily as can the relationships we have with each other. Art, especially the teaching of it to young children, can enrich life by bringing to our attention the quality of such enlivening experiences. There is clearly and inevitably a link between the quality of an experience in art and the quality of life as a result of having had that experience.

A way forward for educators of young children is to persuade colleagues and administrators of the importance of the early years of schooling. A personal view is that within early education, artistic learning has a crucial and indispensable contribution to make. Some educators need no persuading of this. Others wrongly make assumptions about the unsophisticated nature of small children. If we are to improve the quality of art teaching, or for that matter teaching in the early years of schooling, there is still much to be done through in-service work and teachers' groups. Direct experience, such as an in-service course provides, is an increasingly vital part of extending professionalism.

We have experienced increasing emphasis on accountability in teaching and can no longer afford to regard our role as anything else but pro-fessional. We owe it to young children to give them the best art education we possibly can in the short time they are with us. For that reason we need to understand, not only why art education is important for young children, but why early years' education should be given a more prestigious place than it has been.

Dr Lilian Katz, professor of early childhood education at the University of Illinois, has observed on her travels worldwide that the younger the children, the lower the status of teachers seems to be. Yet the most important contribution teachers can make to the education of the young is to make sure they develop the ability to go on wanting to learn. To achieve that requires the greatest of professionalism and expertise, qualities which should place teachers of the young in the highest possible regard.

174

References

APU (1983), *Aesthetic Development* (Assessment of Performance Unit, Department of Education and Science).

Arnheim R. (1966), 'Expression' in Rader M. (ed.), *A Modern Book of Aesthetics*, 3rd ed. (New York: Holt Rinehart & Winston).

Bennett N., Desforges C., Cockburn A. and Wilkinson B., (1984) *The Quality of Pupil Learning Experiences* (London: Lawrence Erlbaum Associates).

Best D. (1983), *The Function and Assessment of Art in Education* (Association of Art Advisors).

Best D. (1985), *Feeling and Reason in the Arts* (London: Allen & Unwin).

De Bono E. (1976), *Teaching Thinking* (London: Penguin).

Dewey J. (1934). *Art as Experience* (New York: Minton, Balch & Co.).

Eberle R. F. (1971), *Scamper: Games for Imagination Development* (New York: Buffalo D.O.K.).

Eisner E. (1972), *Educating Artistic Vision* (London: Collier, Macmillan), Ch. 4−10.

Feldman E. (1982), 'Varieties of Art Curriculum' in *Journal of Art and Design*. Vol. 1, No. 1. (National Society for Art Education).

Field D. (1970), *Change in Art Education* (London: Routledge & Kegan Paul).

Gaitskell C. and Hurwitz A. (1970), *Children and their Art* (New York: Harcourt Brace and World Inc.).

Gardner H. (1980), *Artful Scribbles* (London: Norman Ltd).

Gulbenkian Foundation (1982), *The Arts in Schools* (London: Calhouste Gulbenkian Foundation).

HMI (1978), *Education in England: a survey of H.M. Inspectors of Schools* (London: HMSO).

Hughes R. (1980), *The Shock of the New* (London: BBC Publications).

Jameson K. (1968), *Pre-School and Infant Art* (London: Studio Vista).

Kellogg R. (1969), *Analysing Children's Art* (California: Mayfield Publishing Co.).

Lowenfeld V. and Brittan L. (1970), *Creative and Mental Growth* (New York: Macmillan).

Osborn A. (1948/72), *Your Creative Power; how to use imagination* (New York: Scribner).

Parnes S. and Harding H. (1962), *A Source Book for Creative Thinking* (New York: Scribner).

Perry L. R. (1973), 'Education in the Arts', in Field D. and Newick J. (eds), *The Study of Education and Art* (London: RKP).

Pye D. (1978), *The Nature and Aesthetics of Design* (London: Barrie & Jenkins).

Read H. (1943), *Education Through Art* (New York: Pantheon).

Robertson S. (1974), *Children's Growth Through Creative Experience* (London: Schools Council, Van Nostrand Reinhold).

Ross M. (ed.) (1983), *The Arts: A Way of Knowing* (Oxford: Pergamon).

Rowntree D. (1977), *Assessing Students: How Shall We Know Them?* (London: Harper & Row).

Taylor J. (1971), *Organising and Integrating the Infant Day* (London: Allen & Unwin).

Watts A. (1957), *The Way of Zen* (London: Thames & Hudson).

Witkin R. (1974), *The Intelligence of Feeling* (London: Heinemann).

176

Index

Numbers in *italics* refer to illustrations.